ALEXI KAYE CAMPBELL

Alexi Kaye Campbell's plays include *The Pride* (Royal Court, London, 2008; Lucille Lortel Theatre, New York, 2010; Crucible Theatre, Sheffield, 2011; Trafalgar Studios, 2013); *Apologia* (Bush Theatre, London, 2009; Trafalgar Studios, 2017; Roundabout Theatre, New York, 2018); *The Faith Machine* (Royal Court, London, 2011); *Bracken Moor* (Shared Experience at the Tricycle Theatre, London, 2013) and *Sunset at the Villa Thalia* (National Theatre, London, 2016).

The Pride received the Critics' Circle Award for Most Promising Playwright and the John Whiting Award for Best New Play. The production was also awarded the Laurence Olivier Award for Outstanding Achievement in an Affiliate Theatre.

Alexi's work for film includes *Woman in Gold* (BBC Films and Origin Pictures, 2015).

Other Titles in this Series

Jamie Armitage
A GHOST IN YOUR EAR
AN INTERROGATION

Chiara Atik
POOR CLARE

Annie Baker
THE ANTIPODES
THE FLICK
INFINITE LIFE
JOHN

Mike Bartlett
THE 47TH
ALBION
BULL
GAME
AN INTERVENTION
JUNIPER BLOOD
KING CHARLES III
MIKE BARTLETT PLAYS: TWO
MRS DELGADO
SCANDALTOWN
SNOWFLAKE
UNICORN
VASSA *after* Gorky
WILD

Stephen Beresford
FANNY & ALEXANDER *after* Bergman
THE LAST OF THE HAUSSMANS
THREE KINGS
THE SOUTHBURY CHILD

Caroline Bird
THE LAST STAND OF
   MRS MARY WHITEHOUSE
RED ELLEN

Chris Bush
THE ASSASSINATION OF KATIE HOPKINS
   with Matt Winkworth
THE CHANGING ROOM
CHRIS BUSH PLAYS: ONE
A DOLL'S HOUSE *after* Ibsen
FAUSTUS: THAT DAMNED WOMAN
HUNGRY
JANE EYRE *after* Brontë
THE LAST NOËL
OTHERLAND
ROBIN HOOD AND THE
   CHRISTMAS HEIST
   with Matt Winkworth
ROCK / PAPER / SCISSORS
STANDING AT THE SKY'S EDGE
   with Richard Hawley
STEEL

Jez Butterworth
THE FERRYMAN
THE HILLS OF CALIFORNIA
JERUSALEM
JEZ BUTTERWORTH PLAYS: ONE
JEZ BUTTERWORTH PLAYS: TWO
MOJO
THE NIGHT HERON
PARLOUR SONG
THE RIVER
THE WINTERLING

Alexi Kaye Campbell
ALEXI KAYE CAMPBELL PLAYS: ONE
APOLOGIA
BRACKEN MOOR
THE FAITH MACHINE
THE PRIDE
SUNSET AT THE VILLA THALIA

Sophia Chetin-Leuner
PORN PLAY
SAVE + QUIT
THIS MIGHT NOT BE IT

Caryl Churchill
BLUE HEART
CHURCHILL PLAYS: THREE
CHURCHILL PLAYS: FOUR
CHURCHILL PLAYS: FIVE
CHURCHILL: SHORTS
CLOUD NINE
DING DONG THE WICKED
A DREAM PLAY *after* Strindberg
DRUNK ENOUGH TO SAY I LOVE YOU?
ESCAPED ALONE
FAR AWAY
GLASS. KILL. BLUEBEARD'S FRIENDS.
   IMP.
HERE WE GO
HOTEL
ICECREAM
LIGHT SHINING IN
   BUCKINGHAMSHIRE
LOVE AND INFORMATION
MAD FOREST
A NUMBER
PIGS AND DOGS
SEVEN JEWISH CHILDREN
THE SKRIKER
THIS IS A CHAIR
THYESTES *after* Seneca
TRAPS
WHAT IF IF ONLY

Lucy Kirkwood
BEAUTY AND THE BEAST
   with Katie Mitchell
BLOODY WIMMIN
THE CHILDREN
CHIMERICA
HEDDA *after* Ibsen
THE HUMAN BODY
IT FELT EMPTY WHEN THE HEART
   WENT AT FIRST BUT IT IS
   ALRIGHT NOW
LUCY KIRKWOOD PLAYS: ONE
MOSQUITOES
NSFW
RAPTURE
TINDERBOX
THE WELKIN

Conor McPherson
THE BRIGHTENING AIR
COLD WAR *after* Paweł Pawlikowski
DUBLIN CAROL
GIRL FROM THE NORTH COUNTRY
   with Bob Dylan
McPHERSON PLAYS: ONE
McPHERSON PLAYS: TWO
McPHERSON PLAYS: THREE
THE NEST *after* Franz Xaver Kroetz
THE NIGHT ALIVE
PORT AUTHORITY
THE SEAFARER
SHINING CITY
UNCLE VANYA *after* Chekhov
THE VEIL
THE WEIR

debbie tucker green
BORN BAD
DEBBIE TUCKER GREEN PLAYS: ONE
DIRTY BUTTERFLY
EAR FOR EYE
HANG
NUT
A PROFOUNDLY AFFECTIONATE,
   PASSIONATE DEVOTION TO
   SOMEONE (– *NOUN*)
RANDOM
STONING MARY
TRADE & GENERATIONS
TRUTH AND RECONCILIATION

Alexi Kaye Campbell

BIRD GROVE

NICK HERN BOOKS
London
www.nickhernbooks.co.uk

A Nick Hern Book

Bird Grove first published in Great Britain in 2026 as a paperback original by Nick Hern Books Limited, The Glasshouse, 49a Goldhawk Road, London W12 8QP

Bird Grove © copyright © 2026 Alexi Kaye Campbell

Alexi Kaye Campbell has asserted his moral right to be identified as the author of this work

Cover image: Chronicle / Alamy

Designed and typeset by Nick Hern Books, London
Printed in Great Britain by Mimeo Ltd, Huntingdon, Cambridgeshire PE29 6XX

A CIP catalogue record for this book is available from the British Library

ISBN 978 1 83904 555 4

CAUTION All rights whatsoever in this play are strictly reserved. Requests to reproduce the text in whole or in part should be addressed to the publisher. This book may not be used, in whole or in part, for the development or training of artificial intelligence technologies or systems.

Amateur Performing Rights Applications for performance, including readings and excerpts, by amateurs in the English language throughout the world should be addressed to the Performing Rights Manager, Nick Hern Books, The Glasshouse, 49a Goldhawk Road, London W12 8QP, *tel* +44 (0)20 8749 4953, *email* rights@nickhernbooks.co.uk, except as follows:

Australia: ORiGiN Theatrical, *email* enquiries@originmusic.com.au, *web* www.origintheatrical.com.au

New Zealand: Play Bureau, 20 Rua Street, Mangapapa, Gisborne, 4010, *tel* +64 21 258 3998, *email* info@playbureau.com

United States of America and Canada: David Higham Associates, see details below

Professional Performing Rights Applications for performance by professionals in any medium and in any language throughout the world (and by amateur and stock companies in the United States of America and Canada) should be addressed to David Higham Associates, 6th Floor, Waverley House, 7–12 Noel Street, London W1F 8GQ, *email* nickylund@davidhigham.co.uk

No performance of any kind may be given unless a licence has been obtained. Applications should be made before rehearsals begin. Publication of this play does not necessarily indicate its availability for amateur performance.

www.nickhernbooks.co.uk/environmental-policy

Nick Hern Books' authorised representative in the EU is
Easy Access System Europe – Mustamäe tee 50, 10621 Tallinn, Estonia
email gpsr.requests@easproject.com

Bird Grove was first performed at Hampstead Theatre, London, on 13 February 2026. The cast was as follows:

HORACE GARFIELD	Jonnie Broadbent
ISAAC EVANS	Jolyon Coy
MARY ANN EVANS	Elizabeth Dulau
DOROTHEA	Katie Eldred
CHARLES BRAY	Tom Espiner
CARA BRAY	Rebecca Scroggs
MONSIEUR LAFONTAINE/ HUGO BARING	James Staddon
ROBERT EVANS	Owen Teale
MARIA	Sarah Woodward

Director	Anna Ledwich
Designer	Sarah Beaton
Lighting Designer	Matt Haskins
Sound Designer & Composer	Harry Blake
Co-Composer	Clara Pople
Movement	Chi-San Howard
Casting Director	Juliet Horsley CDG

To Janet

'Family likeness has often a deep sadness in it. Nature, that great tragic dramatist, knits us together by bone and muscle, and divides us by the subtler web of our brains; blends yearning and repulsion; and ties us by our heart-strings to the beings that jar us at every movement.'

George Eliot, Adam Bede

Characters

MARY ANN EVANS, *the young George Eliot, in her twenties*
ROBERT EVANS, *her father, in his sixties*
ISAAC, *her brother, in his thirties*
HORACE GARFIELD, *in his thirties*
MARIA LEWIS, *in her forties*
MONSIEUR LAFONTAINE, *in his fifties*
CHARLES BRAY, *in his fifties*
CARA BRAY, *in her forties*
HUGO BARING, *in his fifties*
DOROTHEA, *in her twenties*

Setting

The play takes place entirely within the walls of Bird Grove, a large, middle-class house on the outskirts of Coventry in the years 1841/42 and 1849.

Bird Grove is a Georgian building.

Five of its ground-floor rooms must be visible to the audience during the play, at some points there are scenes being played simultaneously in more than one of the rooms. At other moments, when we are following the action in one room, the action in the other rooms freezes, and is in shadow.

The five rooms are:

The parlour
The dining room
The kitchen
Robert's study
The entrance hallway, from which the staircase leads to the upstairs floor.

The design for any production of this play does not need to be literal, it can be more abstract, metaphorical.

A little like the house in a memory, or a dream.

This text went to press before the end of rehearsals and so may differ slightly from the play as performed.

ONE

December, 1841.

In darkness, the harmonious sounds of a pastoral idyll: birds tweeting their morning song, the trickle of a running brook, a distant barking of dogs, a horse galloping across a field. A restful, soothing soundtrack.

Then, gradually, it begins to change. The birds start to sound distressed, and the gentle tweeting turns to something more agitated. Then new birds can be heard, predatory ones. Eagles or kestrels swooping down and attacking the robins and blue tits, the violent flapping of wings. The dogs are closer now and turn on each other – savage growling, barking, biting. The horse neighs in terror. A world at war with itself, deafening and terrible.

Then, suddenly, silence.

Lights up.

MARY ANN *stands centre-stage, speaks directly to the audience.*

MARY ANN. Do you not have days when you are aflame with all that you want to say, with all that you want to be? When you feel that all that simmering of mind and soul will reach a boiling point, and then combust and make your head explode? All that blood pulsating through every fibre of your body with these feelings – and your brain bristling with these thoughts!

Before another one arrives, and that other thought chastises you, and points at your egotistical ambition and calls you petty, and proud, and arrogant. For who are you to think you have any power? Who are you, but a plain, inconsequential girl, a provincial nobody, a young woman with ideas above her station in life and foolish dreams to be a writer, a sorry creature who has made the error of filling her mind with too much information, too much knowledge? Who do you think you are, Mary Ann Evans?

ONE 13

We move to Robert's study:

ROBERT *is sitting on a chair, polishing his boots.* ISAAC *hovers a little anxiously, looking out of the window; he is waiting for somebody.*

ROBERT. Your sister has turned her mind to geology.

ISAAC. What on earth can a young woman have to do with geology? It is absurd.

ROBERT. No harm in it.

ISAAC. Unless it hinders her from the main task at hand. Let me remind you, Father, it is the sole reason you came to the area. Why else would one move to Coventry?

ROBERT. The only prospective husband the girl's erudition could intimidate would be a fool, and she deserves better than that.

ISAAC. Which brings me to the reason for my impromptu visit.

ROBERT *is done with the polishing; he bends over and starts to put on his boots, but it isn't easy.*

ROBERT. This Garfield boy.

ISAAC. Horace Garfield is a man, Father, and an excellent match. Is due to come into a substantial fortune. I bumped into him at market the other day, and he asked if he could drop by this afternoon – (*He checks his pocket watch.*) He should be arriving any minute. It is a matter of some urgency, I believe.

ROBERT. But, the timing is not perfect. Help me with my boots, will you, my cursed back.

ISAAC *kneels down, gives him a hand.*

ISAAC. The timing, Father?

ROBERT. We have visitors already. At least, your sister does. The Brays. And they have brought a Frenchman with them, with a beard that almost sweeps the floor.

ISAAC is flabbergasted.

ISAAC. The Brays of Rosehill? Charles Bray, the ribbon manufacturer?

ROBERT. And his wife, Cara, yes.

ISAAC. I must confess, Father, I am astounded that you should invite the Brays to Bird Grove.

ROBERT. Did you not hear what I said? They are your sister's guests.

The boots are on, ROBERT *stands, walks to the mirror.* ISAAC *picks up Robert's waistcoat and jacket, helps him into them.*

You do not like the Brays?

ISAAC. They are extreme freethinkers, Father, and entertain a whole manner of disreputable people at Rosehill, including, I am told from a reliable source, the socialist Robert Owen. If word gets around that Mary Ann is part of their coterie, I believe it would alienate any of the more sensible interested parties and all she'll be left with are Chartists and Radicals. And I don't believe either of those make good husbands.

Waistcoat and jacket are on, ROBERT *takes one last look at himself in the mirror.*

ROBERT. Let us at least try and look respectable.

ISAAC. Let's. But, the timing is most unfortunate, you are correct in that. I do not think that having the Brays and their Frenchman here is helpful to us in the least. Perhaps they will not stay long.

The doorbell rings.

ROBERT. Ah, no doubt that is your eligible young man.

ISAAC. I shall fetch him.

ROBERT. Yes, do that, do that, then bring him in here.

ISAAC. You are too tolerant, Father.

ROBERT *returns one last time to the mirror to comb his hair.* ISAAC *runs into the hallway.* MARY ANN *arrives at exactly the same time from the parlour room; they almost bump into each other.*

MARY ANN. Isaac!

ISAAC. Mary Ann.

MARY ANN. I wonder who it is. You are expecting someone?

ISAAC. No. Yes. I mean, yes, I am.

MARY ANN. Whom are you expecting?

ISAAC. A man. I mean, a friend. A very fine man.

MARY ANN. Well, do join us for tea, if you like, my own friends are here. And very fine men are always welcome!

ISAAC. Splendid.

She is about to return to the parlour room, when he stops her.

Your visitors, how long are they staying, Mary Ann?

MARY ANN. I'm not sure, really. Miss Lewis and myself will be serving tea and the apple cake I made earlier, so a couple of hours I imagine, or thereabouts.

ISAAC. Two hours to eat a slice of apple cake? Are they slow eaters?

MARY ANN. What is the matter, Isaac?

ISAAC. Never mind. Just please ask the Brays to...

MARY ANN. To what, Isaac?

ISAAC. Just to keep to certain subjects... just to discuss, oh I don't know, country walks, that sort of thing. They are big walkers, are they not? They must have lots of local walks to recommend.

MARY ANN. Doubtlessly.

ISAAC. Very good. My guest is always interested in country walks. Excellent!

The doorbell rings again, this time insistently.

Anyway, off you go, I shall open the door.

Perplexed, MARY ANN *returns to the parlour room.*

ISAAC *opens the door, and* HORACE GARFIELD *is standing there, looking somewhat absurd.*

Mr Garfield, how do you do?

HORACE. Not well, I'm afraid, not well at all.

ISAAC. I am sorry to hear it. What is the matter?

HORACE *starts to take his coat, hat, scarf, and gloves off;* ISAAC *takes them one by one and hangs them.*

HORACE. I was passing through Nuneaton last night, on my way back from Elmesthorpe, where I was visiting a cousin who is veritably purple with gout, when I was overcome with ravenous hunger. And so I stopped off at the Wild Boar, do you know it, lovely little inn on the edge of the green, and I indulged in a plate of venison and potatoes. The venison tasted very nice indeed, until about six o'clock this morning, when it decided to take revenge for being eaten. I shall omit the details, only to say it has been a relentless onslaught.

ISAAC. That's most unpleasant for you, perhaps you ought to come back at another time? You must be feeling very uncomfortable.

HORACE. I cannot indulge the luxury of rescheduling, Mr Evans, I am due to meet my father this evening at seven o'clock, and would love to be able to share cheerful news with him. In fact, it is imperative. May I ask where your delightful sister is? Reading and writing, I suspect?

ISAAC. Ah, not quite, in fact she is entertaining some… *acquaintances* of hers in the parlour room, but perhaps it is best if you converse with my father beforehand?

HORACE. Of course, of course, how remiss of me, that is the right way around!

ISAAC. Would you like to... before I introduce you... use the... so you can be more comfortable?

HORACE. A kind offer but I think I will be alright for the time being. Mind over matter, you know.

ISAAC. Yes, of course, but I am sorry about the venison.

HORACE. Let's discuss it no further.

ISAAC. Agreed! Follow me.

And he leads him into Robert's study.

Father, this is Mr Horace Garfield, but I believe you know each other already.

ROBERT. From Trinity, yes, indeed.

ISAAC. This is my father, Robert Evans.

They shake hands, HORACE *vigorously.*

HORACE. It is a delightful church, is it not? And you, sir, are an exemplary sideman.

ROBERT. Thank you, I enjoy it, and it fills my free hours, now that I am retired.

ISAAC. My father is a pillar of the community, a veritable oak.

ROBERT *frees his hand from* HORACE*'s grasp.*

ROBERT. Enough of all that, Mr Garfield, would you care to join me in a drop of whisky, to put you in the festive spirit?

HORACE. It will do me good, Mr Evans, thank you.

ROBERT *walks to the table and pours* HORACE *a whisky, hands it to him.*

I believe your son, sir, may have communicated something of the reason I am here today.

ISAAC. I have, yes.

ROBERT. He has.

HORACE. Marvellous. So we can jump right in.

ROBERT. Into what, sir? A pond?

HORACE. You may be surprised by my urgency.

ROBERT. A little, yes.

HORACE. My father is dying, sir.

ROBERT. Ah, yes, I believe you mentioned that in the summer.

HORACE. He has been dying for the last seven years. But this time it is serious.

ROBERT. I am happy to hear it.

HORACE. I beg your pardon?

ROBERT. No, what I mean is he will no longer be suffering. To suffer for seven years must be a test on his patience. And yours. So for him to be dying at last, after all that dying, will be a relief, I imagine. So, I am happy he will no longer be dying. I mean, suffering.

HORACE. In any case, I am in an unfortunate pickle.

ROBERT. What sort of a pickle?

HORACE. It is to do with my inheritance. My father is in the process of writing a will. He has been preparing it for a few years, now.

ROBERT. Seven, I imagine.

HORACE. And he is of a temperamental character and flexible opinions. So you understand, there have been constant alterations to the document.

ROBERT. That must be a cause of great anxiety to you.

HORACE. I cannot lie, Mr Evans, it is most distressing. Especially the latest draft which is iniquitous and cruel in the extreme.

ROBERT. It is not in your favour?

HORACE. Quite the opposite. It favours my younger brother, Hector, whose name is appropriate to his character. Hector hectors from morning to night, and is a bully to boot. And rapacious for property, and money.

ROBERT. You are not close, then?

HORACE. I loathe the man, but that is by the by. My father is threatening to leave Hector all of his fortune and his estate, Carrington House, which has been in the family since the time of Charles the First.

ROBERT. But you are the first-born.

HORACE. And that is the iniquity. My father, whose days are numbered, I believe –

ROBERT. We'll take his word for it.

HORACE. Is suddenly attaching conditions to his will. Namely, that I shall only be the recipient of my rightful fortune should I find myself a wife and procreate.

ROBERT. So, you are in a hurry to do both.

HORACE. My brother has three children – nasty little brats, I hasten to add – and my father expects me to work towards matching my brother's output.

ROBERT. That should keep you busy.

HORACE. My marriage to a suitable woman would reassure my father that I have begun the process in earnest and hopefully inspire him to alter his will for the final time before his demise and to do so to my advantage.

ROBERT. And this is where my Mary Ann enters the picture.

HORACE. She is a delightful creature. Modest, and well-mannered and altogether perfect for a man like me. I shall look after her, rest assured.

ISAAC. It is a good match, Father.

ROBERT. Allow me though to play the part of devil's advocate.

HORACE. Please.

ROBERT. The impetus of your necessity to find a wife is urgent and compelling.

HORACE. It is.

ROBERT. May not that impetus be colouring your judgement and overwhelming your decision-making? Maybe to the extent that should one introduce you to… oh, I don't know, let's say an available *horse*, a mare I'll grant you, decked in a lace dress, and wearing a string of pearls around her neck, you should be inclined to take her as your wife?

HORACE. Sir!

ISAAC. Father!

ROBERT. I am merely suggesting that your driving need to accomplish your objective in matters of inheritance has perhaps clouded your discernment and persuaded you that my beloved daughter is a good match for you, when indeed there are not many criteria to fulfil the role?

HORACE. Mr Evans, I protest, I am smitten.

ROBERT. You are?

HORACE. How joyful it is when life surprises you. It surprised me when I first laid my eyes on your daughter on the steps of the church.

ROBERT. Did it indeed?

HORACE. All I can say is that it was a miracle, the complete confluence of my economic and romantic aspirations.

ROBERT. We should notify my daughter of this miraculous confluence, as it concerns her.

HORACE. It is the purpose of my visit this afternoon, Mr Evans.

ISAAC. Good man.

HORACE. I am excited by the prospect of articulating my feelings to her. But I am wondering, perhaps, if before I do so, I may after all take up your offer, Mr Evans, of using the… the…

ISAAC. Of course, follow me.

HORACE. Nerves, I expect.

ISAAC. It is most natural.

He leads him out of the study, into the hallway, and opens up the front door of the house.

Round the edge of the house into the garden, you shall spot it under the oak tree, take your time.

HORACE. I may have to. Blasted venison!

And he goes. ISAAC *returns to the study, and* ROBERT.

ISAAC. Your opinion, Father?

ROBERT. I am not altogether sure, Isaac.

ISAAC. With Mary Ann on his arm, he is due to come into a very sizeable fortune.

ROBERT. It is not guaranteed. The irascible father may change his mind yet again and demand that Mary Ann provide triplets before handing it over.

ISAAC. We do not have a choice, Father, there are not suitors lining up, and frankly, she is not for all tastes.

ROBERT. And I am worried about their compatibility. He does not strike me as being particularly serious, and you know your sister.

ISAAC. Opposites attract. And, besides, she is not the romantic type.

ROBERT. Isn't she? Perhaps she has not met the right mate. I feel sometimes there is a deep well of romantic feeling in her that when released will break dams and flood plains.

ISAAC. It must be very deeply underground, Father. The only thing she seems to have any sort of feeling for are books on theological – and now, it appears, *geological* – themes and endless scribbling in her notebooks. The man who will make her content is the one who will allow her to follow both those pursuits, and I believe Horace Garfield will do just that.

ROBERT. He would allow her to be a cannibal should the union persuade the old man to rewrite his will.

He has drifted over to the window; he looks out, becomes ruminative.

Strange girl. Always has been. At least she is over her evangelical phase, it was most intense.

There is a knock on the door.

Enter.

MARIA LEWIS *bursts into the room, in some distress.*

Speaking of evangelicals.

MARIA. Oh, Mr Evans, Isaac, I hope I am not interrupting.

ISAAC. We will be joining you shortly, Miss Lewis.

MARIA. For apple cake, yes, Mary Ann told me. In fact, it is under the pretence of fetching that very apple cake that I have escaped from the parlour room, to come and find you.

ISAAC. Escaped?

ROBERT. What is the matter, Miss Lewis? You seem perturbed.

MARIA. I cannot lie, that I am. Most perturbed. And I wanted to warn you.

ROBERT. Warn us of what?

MARIA. The Frenchman.

ROBERT. What about him?

MARIA. He is a very strange man. And I believe not entirely benign. In fact, quite the opposite.

And she bursts into tears. ISAAC *reaches for a chair, guides her to it.*

ISAAC. Come, sit, Miss Lewis, tell us all.

MARIA. His hands are hovering over Mary Ann, in one of them he is holding a shining fragment of glass and seems to have hypnotised her. He says he is healing her, though whatever it is, it looks like the Devil's work to me.

ISAAC. Healing her of what?

MARIA. Her persistent headaches. And so his hands – the Frenchman's hands – are hovering near her head like a couple of... malevolent ravens.

ISAAC. How ghoulish.

MARIA. We were having a conversation when poor Mary Ann mentioned her crippling headaches, which can often keep her debilitated for days on end.

ROBERT. I know them well.

MARIA. Well, then Monsieur Lafontaine became very excited. He asked Mary Ann to adopt this very unorthodox posture on the chair – she is stretched out on her back like an eagle, and he has thrown himself at her with some zest in his manner.

ROBERT. Eagles, ravens, you are fond of ornithological similes, Miss Lewis.

MARIA. It is all very unusual, and quite alarming.

ISAAC. You did well to warn us, Miss Lewis, we shall enter the room prepared.

The front door opens. HORACE *returns with fresh enthusiasm, and makes his way straight into the study.*

HORACE. I am ready! And feeling hopeful.

ISAAC. Jolly good. Mr Garfield, this is Miss Lewis, my sister's old teacher, and friend, she always stays with us at Christmas, a benevolent influence.

HORACE. How do you do?

MARIA. Mr Garfield.

ISAAC. Right, Father, shall we join Mary Ann, the Frenchman, and the Brays for the business at hand? Mr Garfield, you may have to extract Mary Ann from the room to make your intentions clear with some privacy.

ROBERT. You can bring her in here, if you choose.

HORACE. Thank you, thank you. But did you just mention the Brays?

ISAAC. I did.

HORACE. And they are here? Now? In the parlour room? Your sister is entertaining the Brays?

ISAAC (*in an aside to* ROBERT). Told you, Father.

ROBERT. We are all entertaining the Brays, Mr Garfield. We shall be having tea with them.

MARIA. And apple cake.

HORACE. How very sociable of you. However, there is a problem.

ROBERT. What problem?

HORACE. My parents have advised me against ever talking to them.

ROBERT. Mr Garfield, you are in your thirties, are you not?

HORACE. I am indeed, sir.

ROBERT. But you still follow your parents' advice on whom you should talk to, and whom you should not?

HORACE. Have you met my parents, sir?

ROBERT. I have not had the good fortune.

HORACE. They are very persuasive.

ROBERT. Clearly.

ISAAC. Mr Garfield, be confident that in this house we are not admirers of nefarious dissent. Should the Brays or their French friend provoke or incite, we shall let our thoughts be known with little hesitation. This house and its inhabitants possess a strong moral compass.

HORACE. Your words are comforting, Mr Evans. Very well, I shall make the exception. And after all, my father needn't know about the encounter. We shall be discreet in the matter.

ISAAC *is heading towards the door, leading the others.*

ISAAC. Shall we join them, then?

ROBERT. Yes, let's.

HORACE. Before we do, Mr Evans, may I bother you for one more shot of that delicious whisky? Dutch courage, isn't that what they call it?

ROBERT. To help face my daughter or the Brays?

He fills him up generously; HORACE *downs it in one.* ROBERT *throws* ISAAC *a quick, private look.*

MARIA. And I shall go to the kitchen and fetch the apple cake and the tea.

ISAAC. Do that. We have been warned, Miss Lewis, thank you. Come, let us go.

They all make their way into the hallway; MARIA *heads off into the kitchen;* ISAAC *is about to open the door to the parlour room.*

Please, Mr Garfield, do not let the presence of the Brays derail your intentions. Besides, they are not close to my sister. They hardly know each other.

He enters the parlour room, followed by HORACE *and* ROBERT.

MARY ANN *is stretched out, legs and arms akimbo on a chair, her eyes closed.*

MONSIEUR LAFONTAINE *is standing over her, his hands swaying to and fro, a few inches from her head, a piece of shining glass in his right hand.*

CHARLES BRAY *is standing a few feet away from* MARY ANN *and* LAFONTAINE. *He is watching intently, and taking notes.*

CARA BRAY *is stretched out on the floor with her eyes closed. She is making a deep, moaning noise.*

HORACE. I shall certainly not be telling my father.

LAFONTAINE *brings his finger to his lips, miming a request for silence, he whispers:*

LAFONTAINE. Two minutes, that is all, two minutes!

MARY ANN *is now moaning too, as if she is in ecstasy, or pain.*

ISAAC. Father, this is obscene!

LAFONTAINE. Now breathe in, one last time, Miss Evans, and breathe out. And let it all flow out, all the toxicity, all the poison, let it flow out of you, through your pores and through your cavities and let it all come out, expel it from your body.

His words are having a bad effect on HORACE; *he looks as if he is in physical discomfort, he touches his tummy.*

HORACE (*under his breath, to himself*). Oh, dear.

LAFONTAINE. And now, Miss Evans, you can open your eyes.

He snaps his fingers. MARY ANN *opens her eyes, looking dazed.*

How do you feel, mademoiselle?

MARY ANN. Different. I feel different.

LAFONTAINE. Excellent! And now, we have visitors.

MARY ANN *turns and sees* HORACE, ROBERT *and* ISAAC; *she is taken by surprise and jumps to her feet.* CARA *too is surprised, gets up, and brushes herself down.*

MARY ANN. Oh Father, I am sorry, we got carried away, Monsieur Lafontaine was practising his method on me. Isaac.

CARA. And I couldn't help joining in.

ISAAC. Mary Ann, this is Horace Garfield, I believe you have met before.

MARY ANN. Briefly, at church, yes.

HORACE. Briefly, but unforgettably.

MARY ANN. Mr Garfield is the fine gentleman you were expecting, Isaac?

ISAAC. Yes, indeed. I was singing your praises, Mr Garfield.

MARY ANN. I see.

HORACE. Too kind, too kind.

MARY ANN. Mr Garfield, Father, it is my sincere pleasure to introduce you to Mr and Mrs Charles Bray, and to Mr Lafontaine who is visiting them as part of his national mesmeric tour of Britain.

ISAAC. Lucky Britain.

LAFONTAINE. Enchanté.

ROBERT. How do you do, Mrs Bray, Mr Bray. We have heard so much about you.

CHARLES. I feel like prostrating myself in front of you, sir.

ROBERT. No, please don't, we have seen quite enough already.

CHARLES. To be the father of such a remarkable young woman as Mary Ann can only mean that you too, in turn, are a remarkable human being.

HORACE. Remarkable yes, both of them.

CHARLES. Not far from the tree that bore the apple, and all that.

CARA. Mary Ann has dazzled us, sir, with the force of her intellect and her insatiable curiosity, we love her dearly.

MARY ANN. Cara dear, Mr Bray, please, cease your flattery.

CHARLES. It is not flattery, my dear girl, it is the simple truth.

ROBERT. Please, sit, sit, let us all sit.

He indicates the sofa and chairs which are scattered around the room; they all do as they're told and take a seat.

When they are all seated, there are a few seconds of awkward silence.

It is broken by MARIA *walking in with a tray with the apple cake, plates and spoons on it. Also a teapot, cups and saucers.*

MARIA. I have brought the tea and cake.

MARY ANN. Thank you, Miss Lewis, I shall help you serve it.

She jumps to her feet. For the next couple of minutes MARY ANN *and* MARIA *pour the tea, slice the cake and start handing both out to all in the room.*

I am worried at the size of the cake, it seems to have shrunk in the baking. And I was not expecting Isaac, and his new friend, Mr Garfield.

CHARLES. It is our fault too, we should have notified you that Mr Lafontaine was with us.

ROBERT. You certainly sprung him on us.

MARY ANN. Not at all, Mr Bray, it is our privilege to meet you Monsieur Lafontaine. But the cake slices will be very thin, I'm afraid.

ISAAC. Mr Lafontaine, do explain, please, what it was that you were just now subjecting my sister to.

MARY ANN. I was not being subjected to anything, Isaac, I was a willing participant. In fact, it was I who volunteered to be treated by Monsieur Lafontaine.

ROBERT. I do not doubt it, Mary Ann, of late you seem enthusiastic for novel experiences. But please do explain your method, we are fascinated.

LAFONTAINE. From a young age I discovered I had a gift, monsieur, a vocation if you prefer, to be able to lead people into a state where… how can I describe it… they are susceptible to my influence.

HORACE. What a marvellous gift.

LAFONTAINE. Quite simply, I am a hypnotist, and when my patients are in the state of hypnosis under my spell, I find that they are immune to physical discomfort and that also, they are sometimes able to heal themselves of certain chronic conditions. All living beings on this planet are mere vessels of life, perhaps, but alas, those poor, wretched vessels can cause us so much misery and pain.

HORACE. Indeed, at times one feels it acutely.

CHARLES. But it is not only us humans who fall under Monsieur Lafontaine's mesmerising influence. Last week, to great fanfare and excitement, he hypnotised a lion at London Zoo.

ROBERT. Oh, you are in good company, Mary Ann.

LAFONTAINE. But my only real wish is that I can use my talent for the betterment of life and to alleviate suffering wherever I find it.

CHARLES. What a noble cause.

CARA. Wonderful, wonderful!

LAFONTAINE. Let us hope, mademoiselle, that your migraines will torture you no more.

MARY ANN. That would be a fine outcome.

A slight pause; they are all now enjoying their tea and cake.

HORACE. Your apple cake is delicious, Miss Evans, it melts in the mouth. You too have gifts, it appears, though perhaps not quite as unusual as those of Mr Lafontaine.

MARY ANN. Thank you, Mr Garfield.

ISAAC. Mary Ann is a very fine cook, she has also mastered cheese-making, preserves, plucking birds, baking, laundering, and general housekeeping to the most outstanding degree, has she not, Father?

CARA. That sounds like a personal advertisement from *The Birmingham Journal*, Mr Evans.

ROBERT. She is the reason I no longer employ a housekeeper.

CARA. How you manage all that, my dear, along with giving yourself the finest self-education of any woman I know, is quite a mystery to me, there are only so many hours in the day.

MARY ANN. But then there is the night, Cara, and candlelight.

The two women smile at each other, a little conspiratorially.

ISAAC. So, really, Mr Lafontaine, you consider yourself something of a Christ figure?

MARY ANN. Isaac!

LAFONTAINE. Do I?

MARIA. That is blasphemous, Isaac.

HORACE. That Christ should be a Frenchman, you mean?

ISAAC. Going around the country healing people, and lions.

LAFONTAINE. I think you misheard me, sir. I did not say I healed them. I said, that under my influence, they heal *themselves*. But yes, I suppose I have that in common with Jesus, in that he too was trying to inspire people to do just that. 'Heal thyself!', isn't that his most persistent incantation? So maybe I am trying, in all humility, to do the same.

ISAAC. There is nothing humble in comparing yourself to the son of God, sir.

LAFONTAINE. I believe, monsieur, that the comparison was introduced by yourself.

MARY ANN. You are correct, Monsieur Lafontaine, it was.

LAFONTAINE. But even so, what is blasphemous about that comparison, Miss Lewis? After all, are we not all the children of God? Isn't that what the wonderful story is trying to tell us, perhaps to point us like a magical fairy tale towards our higher selves, and suggest something of what we are capable of? Our dormant powers.

MARIA. Fairy tale?

ISAAC. I have to be honest and say that I find what you are saying offensive, Mr Lafontaine. And, what's more, the sight – when we opened the door just now – of yourself, standing like some... deranged demon, if you'll pardon me, over my sister, swaying to and fro, holding that wretched piece of glass in your hand – well, the sight was, quite frankly, disturbing to me in the extreme.

CHARLES. Only because it is something you have never seen before.

HORACE. None of us have. Not in the Midlands, anyway.

Pause.

CHARLES. I hope you are not offended, young Mr Evans, when I say you remind me a little of my dog.

CARA. Charles.

ISAAC. Offended? Not in the least.

CHARLES. Good. I would hate to cause offence. He is a very fine dog, so it is a flattering comparison, I assure you.

ISAAC. I'm assured, then.

CHARLES. Of course, there is a very real comfort in tradition.

HORACE. Tradition?

ISAAC. How am I like your dog, pray?

CHARLES. Voltaire is a Pyrenean Mountain Dog, noble, like yourself, handsome, like yourself, and very protective of those he loves, like you are protective of your sister, Mr Evans, it is most touching. So yes, there are many similarities. And perhaps one more.

ISAAC. And what is that?

CHARLES. He does not like the unfamiliar, either. Simply, because it is unfamiliar.

ISAAC. I do not understand you.

CHARLES. Even though that unfamiliar element, whatever it may be, may well be bringing him an improvement to his life, the promise of future happiness. Let me give you an example – perhaps a stranger is knocking on our door on a stormy winter's night. Voltaire will growl and bark and if unleashed, when the door is opened, he will leap onto the man to bite him viciously, maybe even draw blood. But perhaps that poor man is holding in his hands a bowl of the most delicious cooked beef, which he is bringing Voltaire and which Voltaire would love more than anything in the world. But the silly dog would be more preoccupied by the imagined threat of the unfamiliar man than he would be of the delicious feast that very man is ready to offer him.

ISAAC. I am not following you.

CHARLES. Look at us, will you. We have thousands of years of history behind us and what have they left us – fields scattered with the burnt, skewered, bloodied and beheaded bodies of a billion men, a billion souls. But the sight of Monsieur Lafontaine trying with good heart to ease the pain of your sister by waving his arms around her head in a strange fashion, that is what fills you with apprehension and dread!

MARY ANN. And likewise – just because something is familiar, maybe has been since the dawn of our existence, it does not mean that it is necessarily what is best for us, isn't that correct?

CHARLES. We have much more in common with my beloved Voltaire than we may like to think.

MARY ANN. I have never heard a simpler and more accurate description of our natural proclivity to conservatism, Mr Bray.

ROBERT. And you've certainly put my son in his place.

ISAAC. Well, there is only one reply I have to that.

CHARLES. And what is that, Mr Evans?

ISAAC. Woof, woof!

Laughter all around, but the tension is there. MARIA *has stood and is about to pour some more tea into* ROBERT's *cup but the pot has run dry.*

MARIA. Oh, dear, there is no more tea left, and we have run out of cake as well.

MARY ANN *stands*.

MARY ANN. I shall replenish the teapot and I shall butter some bread, I'm so sorry the cake was so small.

CHARLES. Delicious, though.

ISAAC *throws* HORACE *a look;* HORACE *jumps to his feet.*

HORACE. I shall accompany you, Miss Evans.

MARY ANN. Don't be ridiculous, Mr Garfield, I will do it on my own.

HORACE. I insist, I shall come and assist you.

MARY ANN. I do not require any assistance, Mr Garfield. It will only take me a minute, I shall fill up the teapot and butter a few slices of bread.

HORACE. I enjoy buttering.

MARY ANN. That is neither here nor there, Mr Garfield, I insist you remain here.

ISAAC. Accept his kind offer with good grace, Mary Ann.

MARY ANN. Alright then, Mr Garfield. Thank you for your kind offer. Do come and help me butter the bread, if you must.

CARA *reads* MARY ANN, *jumps to her feet.*

CARA. Buttering is a woman's task, you shall do no such thing, Mr Garfield. It is I who will fetch the tea with Miss Evans and butter the bread.

HORACE. It has been decided that it shall be me who will help Miss Evans with the buttering, Mrs Bray.

CARA. I will not accept it! Sit down, Mr Garfield, and finish your tea!

HORACE. I shan't, Mrs Bray.

CARA *becomes forceful.*

CARA. Sit down, please, Mr Garfield! I insist that I shall go with Mary Ann to the kitchen. No more arguing!

He does as he's told; sits, sulkily.

Thank you. Come on, my dear, let us go fetch the tea and bread.

CARA *leads out of the parlour room.* MARY ANN *follows her, with the teapot.*

HORACE. Your wife is a forceful character, Mr Bray.

CHARLES. Only when she feels the necessity.

ISAAC. You give up too easily, Mr Garfield.

A slight pause.

ROBERT. But your friendship with my daughter is a new one, I believe, Mr Bray. You do not know her very well.

CHARLES. It's true, we have only known Mary Ann since you moved to Bird Grove earlier this year, sir. But I am happy to report she has pursued our friendship with vigour and intensity.

ISAAC. Has she indeed?

ROBERT. I know she's visited you at Rosehill a couple of times.

CHARLES. More than a couple, Mr Evans, more like seven or eight.

HORACE. How interesting.

ROBERT. When she is out on her long walks, I expect.

CHARLES. Indeed, to our delight, she always drops in.

HORACE. I see.

ROBERT. I had no idea.

MARIA. Both you and your wife have made a very deep impression on her, Mr Bray. Her letters to me are full of passionate descriptions of the myriad conversations you have had at Rosehill, on subjects far and wide.

ROBERT. I've been too busy to notice, I expect.

ISAAC. It seems so, Father.

CHARLES. Rosehill seems to attract people like your daughter, Mr Evans, and when like minds meet, conversation, of course, is inevitable, and hopefully, fruitful.

ONE 35

LAFONTAINE. The reputation of your house, Mr Bray, has even reached Paris.

HORACE. Is that a good thing?

ROBERT. And what are some of those subjects? She keeps them to herself, so I am not informed.

CHARLES. Your daughter has been quite taken by the work of my wife's brother, Mr Charles Hennell, and in particular his book *An Inquiry Concerning the Origin of Christianity*.

ISAAC. Your wife's brother? You are quite a family, you are everywhere!

HORACE. Like an octopus.

ROBERT. A theological book, yes, she likes those.

CHARLES. She's learnt whole paragraphs by heart.

LAFONTAINE. Incroyable!

MARIA. She hasn't mentioned that one. And why is an inquiry even necessary, I ask myself.

CHARLES. And only last week we were in rapt conversation about John Smith's *The Relation Between the Holy Scriptures and Some Parts of Geological Science*.

ISAAC. Sounds a riveting read.

MARIA. What a peculiar title.

ROBERT. Ah, yes, geology, her new passion.

MARIA. But what has geology to do with the Holy Scriptures, may I ask?

CHARLES. Ah, Miss Lewis, that is a big question.

MARIA. And one, perhaps, that I wouldn't want answered.

Pause.

ISAAC. And what is the merit of it all, I wonder.

CHARLES. The merit?

ISAAC. There are inquiries and there are inquiries. And, as Miss Lewis just rightly pointed out, one wonders if each and every inquiry is useful and beneficial to the improvement of our lot.

HORACE. Especially if the inquirer is a young woman.

CHARLES. You do not believe, Mr Garfield, in the education of women?

HORACE. To a point, to a point. But that point does not reach as far as the relationship between religion and geometry.

ISAAC. Geology.

HORACE. Geology.

CHARLES. I see.

ROBERT is lost in thought, he is weighing things up.

In the kitchen, MARY ANN *and* CARA *are slicing bread and buttering it, and water is being heated for the teapot.*

MARY ANN. I'll cut a few more slices, Cara, why don't you please get started by buttering those ones there?

CARA. I'll do that.

A pause as they take to their tasks – MARY ANN *slicing,* CARA *buttering.*

MARY ANN. Mr Bray's dog analogy was entertaining.

CARA. Did you really think so, my dear?

MARY ANN. Oh, you were smiling, so I thought you enjoyed it.

CARA. I smile a lot when Charles is talking, have you not noticed?

MARY ANN. Now that you mention it.

CARA. I just play along, to keep him happy. We do that all the time, don't we? With our husbands, our fathers, our brothers. We prop them up, do we not, my dear?

MARY ANN. Yes, I suppose we do.

CARA. Oh, don't get me wrong, he's a very clever man, Charles, and I adore him. But he seems to need constant affirmation of his cleverness. So I nod, and smile, and play my part.

MARY ANN. Play your part?

CARA. You'll come to see it more and more.

Pause.

Do you know, I think we are a little like very fine performers in a theatrical play, Mary Ann.

MARY ANN. A theatrical play?

CARA. And the play itself, of course, has been penned by a man.

MARY ANN. I hadn't thought of it that way.

CARA. Because it's all about who's telling the stories, isn't it? I think of that often.

MARY ANN. Telling the stories?

CARA. The stories that shape our lives, and shape the world. You read your Walter Scott, my darling, and your Shakespeare, and your Bible, of course. And all those stories – whether you believe the last to be factual or not – have been written by a small pool of men – *are* written by those men, and probably *will* be written by those men, for a very long time to come. And of course those men should be able to write their stories, and create landscapes and worlds, and kingdoms, and whatnot, I would never expect them to stop doing that, telling stories is what makes sense of the world, or at least tries to, and it's everyone's right. But as long as you only have one sort of person telling the stories, well then our world will just end up looking very like that one sort of person. It makes sense, doesn't it? These are finished, shall I put them on the plate?

MARY ANN. Yes, please.

CARA *places the buttered slices on the large plate, and wipes her hands on a tea towel.*

I wonder why we have sat back and accepted it so readily.

CARA. Because if you take someone by the hand, my dear, and sit them down, and tell them in a very forceful and persuasive voice, that they are foolish, and weak, and limited, and you do that day in and day out, for weeks, and months, and years, and centuries, that someone will come to believe those words as if they are an irrefutable truth.

MARY ANN. Of course they will.

HORACE *enters the kitchen but they do not see him; he hovers by the door.*

CARA. But let me tell you a secret. We are *not* foolish, and we are *not* limited. And we are certainly not weak. In fact, I suspect we are stronger. But our strength is different to theirs.

MARY ANN. So then, I suppose, it is time for us to wrestle the pen from their hands, and at least share in the storytelling.

CARA. Grabbing that pen will be your duty.

MARY ANN. My *duty*.

HORACE *clears his throat.*

CARA. The bread has been buttered, Mr Garfield, and we are about to return to the parlour room. So there is nothing left for you to do.

HORACE. I have come to speak to Miss Evans.

CARA. Well, we can all return to the parlour room together, and you may speak to her there.

HORACE. In private.

A pause.

MARY ANN. It is fine, Cara, why don't you take the bread and serve the others and Mr Garfield and I shall join you presently. I'll bring the tea, the water is nearly boiled.

CARA. Are you sure, my dear?

HORACE. Worry not, Mrs Bray, I have no plans to eat her.

CARA. I'm sure we're all thankful for that, Mr Garfield.

HORACE. Just to converse.

MARY ANN. Run along, Cara.

CARA. If you insist.

CARA picks up the tray with the plate of buttered bread on it, and leaves the room. MARY ANN starts to fill the teapot with the water which has boiled.

MARY ANN. How can I help you, Mr Garfield?

HORACE. I need to speak to you.

MARY ANN. I believe we have established that already. But what, may I ask, is the subject?

HORACE. You are, Miss Evans. And I am. *We* are.

MARY ANN. I do not understand you.

HORACE. Miss Evans, may I speak frankly?

MARY ANN. If you must.

HORACE. Oh, I do, I do.

MARY ANN. Well, proceed then.

HORACE. Ever since I first spotted your beauty on the steps of Trinity Church –

MARY ANN. I'm afraid I'm going to have to stop you right there, Mr Garfield.

HORACE. But I haven't even started, Miss Evans.

MARY ANN. Oh, but you have, Mr Garfield, and most inauspiciously. And dishonestly.

HORACE. Dishonestly?

MARY ANN. I am guilty of both arrogance and self-delusion, Mr Garfield, in matters far and wide. Apart from when it comes to my physical appearance. I am allowed no space for indulging either of those vices in relation to that particular field. There are many qualities I like, in my more conceited moments, to believe I possess, but natural beauty has never been nor can ever be one of them.

HORACE. I protest.

MARY ANN. You can protest all you like that the world is flat when we know for a fact that it is not.

HORACE. Beauty is in the eye of the beholder, Miss Evans.

MARY ANN. Well, then in this particular case, the beholder is either blind or deranged. Continue.

HORACE. Well, anyway, as I was saying, since I first spotted you –

MARY ANN. That's better.

HORACE. On the steps of Trinity Church, I have thought of little else.

MARY ANN. How unfortunate for you.

HORACE. And have come here today, to announce my ardent affection for you, and to also ask if you would even consider…

He starts, with some difficulty, to get down onto one knee; she stops him.

MARY ANN. Please, sir, desist!

HORACE. But I don't want to.

MARY ANN. Mr Garfield, please restrain yourself, until I have spoken.

He stops, pulls himself up again.

HORACE. Speak, then, Miss Evans, you have my ears.

MARY ANN. Thank you. I do not mean to offend you, sir, when I state that I believe any proposal you are here to make – matrimonial or otherwise – is nothing short of premature. We have met only three times on the steps of the church and on each occasion I believe we had conversations pertaining to nothing more than the weather.

HORACE. Indeed. But on the second of those occasions, there was an imminent storm.

MARY ANN. The meteorological details are insignificant, Mr Garfield.

HORACE. And the conversation we shared on the subject of that arriving storm, was poetical, and dare I say it, on your side, metaphorical.

MARY ANN. If I was the guilty party in introducing poetry and what I'm sure was laborious metaphor into that conversation –

HORACE. You were, but it was not laborious, it was thrilling.

MARY ANN. Then I can only apologise.

HORACE. Whatever for?

MARY ANN. For leading you up the garden path, whatever the weather, and whatever the metaphor.

HORACE. Miss Evans.

MARY ANN. Mr Garfield.

HORACE. Allow me to interrogate the wording you just used.

MARY ANN. What wording?

HORACE. You just described my overtures as premature.

MARY ANN. In the extreme.

HORACE. Not as erroneous, not as misjudged, but simply as premature.

MARY ANN. Oh, dear, yes, I see where you are going with this.

HORACE. The use of that particular word inspires my patience, but also my hope.

MARY ANN. No, Mr Garfield, it should inspire neither.

HORACE. And with that in mind, I would like to ask you a favour.

MARY ANN. What favour?

HORACE. That you accompany me tonight to meet my father.

Pause.

He is on his deathbed.

MARY ANN. I am very sorry to hear it, Mr Garfield. But what good can come from the introduction?

HORACE. It would bring him comfort in his last days.

MARY ANN. I believe the last thing the poor man needs as he is about to slip away into eternity, is to be introduced to some strange woman with whom he has absolutely no relation, or connection.

HORACE. I will tell him the opposite. That we do, in fact, have a connection. And that one day, very soon, I will have the joy of calling you my beloved wife.

MARY ANN. But that would be a terrible lie, Mr Garfield, and to lie to a dying man I feel is even more sinful than lying to one in the throes of life.

Pause.

Mr Garfield, again, I do not wish to insult or upset you. But your resolve demands my frankness. I will instruct you to take any hopes, dreams, and wishes that you may be harbouring towards my person, to pack them away in a chest, to lock the chest, to throw away the key, and then to bury the chest somewhere from whence it can never be salvaged, not even in a million years, when perhaps the human race will no longer be inhabiting this planet. Do I make myself clear?

HORACE. No.

Pause.

Because the surprise I feel at your rejection of me overwhelms the credibility of your position.

MARY ANN. Does it really?

HORACE. I believe you are making a very foolish choice, Miss Evans, which you will regret bitterly with time. And one that will disappoint both your father and brother.

MARY ANN. Why do you say that?

HORACE. Because they were both enthusiastic supporters of my intentions.

MARY ANN. Were they indeed?

A pause as she takes this on board.

Shall we return to the parlour room for more tea? And let us talk no more on the subject.

HORACE. I shall join you shortly. I need to… go for a walk in the garden. To expunge the disappointment.

MARY ANN. As you wish.

MARY ANN *picks up the teapot and leaves the kitchen with* HORACE *in tow.* MARY ANN *makes her way to the parlour room;* HORACE *leaves through the front door to the garden, and relief.*

In the parlour, the conversation is in full flow, and getting more heated.

ISAAC. Because society, sir, follows the rules of Nature. And Nature dictates that men are the more dominant sex, women the more submissive.

CHARLES. There are biological differences, of course there are, and yes, there is a physical strength in men that is usually lacking in women, I will grant you that.

ISAAC. Thank you for granting me the obvious, Mr Bray.

CHARLES. But that strength, my dear man, is in the arms and not the mind, the legs and not the heart.

CARA. Alas, it is the strength in those arms that has determined that men should rule, through the violent use of them, or simply the threat of that use.

CHARLES. But we are on the cusp of great and monumental change, Mr Evans. Machines, sir, will alter the very fabric of our world, and the way it works. And so those qualities of physical strength, which have rendered men the more powerful, will perhaps, with time, become obsolete. And then, sir, the call will be on us.

ISAAC. What call?

CHARLES. The call to change, Mr Evans, the call to *evolve*.

MARY ANN *enters the room with the teapot.*

ROBERT. And here she is.

MARY ANN. I have brought the tea.

She goes from person to person, filling up their cups with the hot brew.

Your friend Mr Garfield is in the garden, Father, getting some fresh air, he looked as if he needed it.

ROBERT. He is your brother's friend, Mary Ann, not mine.

MARY ANN. Be that as it may, I have made my feelings clear to him.

ROBERT. Jolly good. I suspected you would.

ISAAC. I hope you have not responded in haste, Mary Ann.

MARY ANN. I have certainly responded, Isaac.

She has finished with the pouring of the tea; she sits.

I am sorry, I did not mean to interrupt the conversation.

CHARLES. I believe it had reached its natural conclusion, Miss Evans. A conclusion in which your brother and I will beg to differ.

ISAAC. And probably not only on that one issue.

CARA. Your timing was fortuitous, my dear. It is three days before Christmas, and not the time for arguments, but for peace, and understanding. Even though, perhaps, we do not always see the world with the same eyes.

MARIA. It is my favourite time of year. I am full of gratitude for the birth of our Lord Jesus Christ, who brought light into this dark, dark world.

ROBERT. Indeed, Miss Lewis, indeed.

HORACE *meanwhile has returned from the garden; he sneaks into Robert's study, pours himself one more large glass of whisky, and again, downs it in one.*

In the parlour room, the conversation continues.

But will you allow me a thought?

CHARLES. We are keen to hear it, sir.

ROBERT. I am not a well-educated man, nor am I intellectual, or particularly well-informed. I have been an estate manager all my life and have learnt about the digging of ditches, and the thatching of roofs, and the tilling of fields.

CHARLES. The best knowledge, and the most important.

ROBERT. And I hear what you say about our similarity to dogs, Mr Bray, and our wariness of the new, and the unfamiliar. But there is also much which has painstakingly been put together over the centuries, a little in the same and meticulous way the thatcher has woven those very roofs, which has been created to bring some order to our world, and structure, and to stop the weather getting in. It is no mean feat, sir.

CHARLES. Indeed, it isn't.

ROBERT. Progress is all very good, but not if it wrecks everything on its bold, determined way, because surely on that path it drives down in its earnest will to transform the world, there are certain things of value, and worth, and lasting significance. Things that have been created for a reason, even though that reason may not always be clear to us. So, we should proceed with caution, no?

CHARLES. It is indeed a delicate balance, Mr Evans.

And then HORACE *is back in the parlour room, fuelled by his latest shot of whisky.*

HORACE. Mr Evans, Mr Evans, I shall bother you no longer, my task here is done, and I shall be departing this house and heading to my father's. Your daughter has made her feelings clear to me in a most unequivocal way.

CHARLES. Feelings on what?

ROBERT. I'm afraid Mary Ann certainly knows her mind, Mr Garfield.

MARY ANN. I am beginning to.

HORACE. Oh, yes, sir, be very afraid, because no good can come of it, mark my words.

ROBERT. Proceed with caution, Mr Garfield.

HORACE. I think it is you, sir, who should proceed with the caution which you warn me with. It is clear that your daughter is taking a dangerous path in life, and one, I fear, that will cause you much consternation.

CHARLES. What has caused this outburst?

CARA. Rejection, I believe.

ROBERT. Mr Garfield, the desperation of your situation is driving you to behave in an unseemly manner, I think you should try and temper yourself. It is not my daughter's fault that you have until this evening to do what you can to salvage any likelihood of a legacy.

HORACE. It is clear to me, from the way that she expressed herself just now, that she has come under the influence of pernicious forces. And, as it happens, those forces are in this very room, enjoying tea and buttered bread.

CHARLES. Good Lord.

HORACE. Good Lord indeed, sir, though in your mouth those two holy words sound disingenuous, and dare I say it, blasphemous.

CHARLES. This is really quite outrageous.

ROBERT. I suggest it is time you left my house, sir.

HORACE. I will second that opinion, and with some enthusiasm. I would rather remain in a house of vipers, adders, and... other poisonous creatures.

ISAAC. There's no need for that, Garfield.

ROBERT. Let me see you out.

HORACE. With pleasure, with great pleasure.

He heads for the door, then stops, turns to MARY ANN *with dramatic flair.*

You were right to correct me, Miss Evans, when I complimented you on your looks. There is little beauty there, inside or out.

ROBERT. SILENCE, SIR!

HORACE. I doubt you will ever find yourself a respectable husband. Goodnight to you.

MARY ANN. You may well be right. Goodnight, Mr Garfield.

ROBERT. This way. NOW.

And he leads him to the hallway, and to the front door. Everyone in the parlour room has been shocked into silence.

ROBERT *opens the door, and* HORACE *reels out;* ROBERT *shouts out after him.*

A word of advice, Mr Garfield! A few hundred feet down the road on the left, is a field. It is where my neighbour keeps his two nags. You may want to stop and propose to one of them. But I wouldn't get your hopes up!

He turns, and drifts away from the door, lost in thought, and shaken. The door is kept open.

He wanders into his study, trying to take on board the afternoon, the conversations, the situation.

In the parlour room, too, they are still reeling.

LAFONTAINE. I am surprised. I thought the English never make a scene.

CHARLES. Rarely, Mr Lafontaine. But when they do, they put their heart into it.

MARY ANN. Will Mr Garfield remain your friend, Isaac?

ISAAC. You know he won't. But it is clear that his behaviour is the result of strong feelings and not a faithful indication of his character.

CARA. Is behaviour not character, Mr Evans?

MARY ANN. You do me wrong, Isaac.

Pause. Then suddenly, the gentle, almost ethereal sound of a young boy's beautiful alto voice, singing.

It is coming from the front door of the house, which ROBERT *has left ajar.*

MARIA. Listen!

They do just that. The solitary voice is joined by a baritone, and then a tenor. The effect is soothing, and numinous.

ROBERT *slowly drifts towards the door, and opens it wide.*

One young boy, and two older ones, and their simple instruments, are performing a Christmas carol. Perhaps we can see them, perhaps not. But we can hear the power of their song.

CHARLES. It is the 'Coventry Carol'.

MARIA. My favourite.

CARA. What voices. Like angels.

From the hallway, ROBERT *calls.*

ROBERT. Carols!

LAFONTAINE. Wonderful!

MARIA. Let us go and listen!

MARIA *runs out of the parlour room, followed by the* BRAYS *and* LAFONTAINE, *and* ISAAC. *Before he leaves the room, he throws a last look at* MARY ANN.

MARY ANN *does not move. She remains in the room, wrapped in thought, and staring ahead.*

The rest of the group all congregate around the front door, listening to the carol.

But halfway through it, CARA *turns, and notices that* MARY ANN *has not joined them.*

She walks back to the parlour room and finds MARY ANN *now weeping gently.*

CARA. Oh, my darling, what is the matter?

MARY ANN *does not reply; her weeping continues, and increases.*

Don't let those cruel words upset you. The man was an imbecile.

MARY ANN. It is not the reason I am crying, Cara.

CARA. Then, what is?

A pause before MARY ANN *answers.*

MARY ANN. It is because I know what I need to do.

And then quietly, but resolutely, almost to herself:

I know what I need to do.

The lights fade to darkness.

TWO

It is ten days later, the 3rd of January, 1842.

Early morning, and it is snowing. Through the windows we can see the white powder falling heavily, continuously.

In the dining room, the fire is lit.

MARY ANN *and* MARIA *are in the kitchen, preparing breakfast.*

Then suddenly, MARIA *drops a bowl of oats; it breaks and shatters into pieces. She lets out a cry.*

MARIA. Oh, no. I don't know what is the matter with me this morning.

MARY ANN. Do not worry yourself, there are more oats, I'll fetch them. But first, we need to clean up the mess.

MARIA. Third thing I have dropped.

MARY ANN. It is your hands, they are shaking.

MARIA. My nerves, I expect.

MARY ANN. Well, you must try and pull yourself together, my dear. Why don't you stand aside, and let me do it.

MARIA *does as she's told and goes and stands by the window; looks out.*

MARY ANN *gets a brush and dustpan, gets on her knees and starts to clear up the mess of the broken bowl and the spilt oats.*

MARIA. It's turning into a blizzard out there, everything is covered, the path will be treacherous, and slippery.

MARY ANN. You have your boots.

MARIA. Maybe your father will not want to go to church in this weather.

MARY ANN. He is the sideman, Miss Lewis. He shall go to church even if the world collapses.

MARIA. I feel as if it is about to do just that.

And she turns to MARY ANN.

And I beg you to reconsider.

MARY ANN. Miss Lewis. We have spoken about this already, and I have told you, today is the day. I am not going back. Not now.

MARIA. I thought that when we had discussed it on Boxing Day, that perhaps I had dissuaded you.

MARY ANN. I said not a word to give you that impression, so it must have been wishful thinking on your part.

MARIA. You were very quiet after our conversation, and I assumed that maybe you were having second thoughts.

MARY ANN. I was quiet because I became more resolved than ever, and I came to see that I would not persuade you. So it seemed a waste of my time to try.

MARIA. I could not be persuaded by such a decision. It is wrong.

And she begins to weep.

MARY ANN. I was hoping that you would be able to support me today.

MARIA. How can I support you if I don't agree with you?

MARY ANN. Because you have been my teacher and my friend, for many years. You do not need to be in accordance with my every choice to be able to stand by my side and hold my hand as I make it.

MARIA. As your friend and your teacher, it is my duty to speak my opinion.

MARY ANN. And yet you condemn me for wanting to do the same.

MARIA. Because I believe that opinion to be wicked.

MARY ANN. Only because you do not agree with it.

MARIA. No one will agree with it, Mary Ann. And you will be shunned and hated for it.

MARY ANN. Then let me be shunned and hated.

The mess has been cleared. MARY ANN *stands.*

Right, let us begin again. I shall cook the porridge. Could you please see to the tea, instead? My father will be down any minute and he will want his breakfast, and his morning tea.

MARY ANN *begins cooking and stirring the porridge. And* MARIA *boils water and makes the tea. All this happens over the next few moments of the scene.*

MARIA. I would like to ask you the same question I did on Boxing Day.

MARY ANN. And I will no doubt answer it in the same manner, nothing has changed since then.

MARIA. But it is something that I cannot get out of my head. That these are not your own thoughts, but that they have been planted there.

MARY ANN. By the Brays, no doubt. But you do me a great disservice by suggesting that I do not form my own thoughts and that I am so indelibly shaped by those of others. I thought you knew me better.

MARIA. And so did I. But these thoughts are so out of character, so yes, I cannot but think that you have been unduly influenced.

MARY ANN. Well, I suppose, yes, I have been. Influenced by every encounter, by every debate, by every single line of every single book I have ever read. Only those who cling stubbornly to one, monolithic way of looking at the world will fail to be influenced by other views. One listens, one is open, and then when one has heard all of the conflicting standpoints, one forms their own. Is that not the right way? Anything else is to be in a state of semi-slumber. So yes, I suppose you are right, I *have* been influenced.

She walks into the hallway, and shouts upstairs.

Father! Your breakfast is nearly ready!

She walks back into the kitchen.

Why don't you take a moment to compose yourself? If you cannot stand by my side at this significant juncture, perhaps I could at least ask you not to add to its difficulty? I shall finish preparing the breakfast on my own.

MARIA. As you wish.

She starts to make her way out of the room, but pauses before she leaves.

I have known you since you were a child.

MARY ANN. So maybe in your eyes, I remain one. Or, you prefer me to remain one.

MARIA. That isn't what I was going to say.

MARY ANN. What, then?

MARIA. I love you inordinately, my dear girl. It is only my very profound concern that drives me to try and stop you from a course of action which I fear will have devastating consequences.

MARY ANN. Then I shall have to bear them.

MARIA. But perhaps you will not be the only one.

And she leaves the room and walks into the parlour room. Once there, she kneels on the floor, against an armchair, and starts a quite fervent prayer, reciting the Lord's Prayer under her breath, over and over.

MARY ANN *walks back into the hallway and shouts upstairs once more.*

MARY ANN. Father! You will be late!

She then returns to the kitchen, stirs the porridge one last time, and begins to pour it into three bowls.

ROBERT *comes down the stairs into the hallway, dressed in his Sunday best for church. He then makes his way into the dining room, and sits at his usual place, at the head of the table.*

MARY ANN *puts the three bowls of porridge onto a tray, and also the teapot. She then carries it all into the dining room.*

Good morning, Father.

ROBERT. Good morning, Mary Ann.

MARY ANN. Did you sleep well?

ROBERT. Well enough.

MARY ANN. I have made porridge. It will warm you on this cold day.

She places the tray onto the table, which has already been set. She puts Robert's porridge down in front of him, then one bowl each in Maria's place, and her own. Then she picks up the teapot and pours their three cups of tea, starting with her father's. She does the same with a jug of milk. Throughout this ritual, MARIA *remains in the next room, praying.*

Eventually, MARY ANN *walks to the door of the dining room, and calls her.*

Miss Lewis! Breakfast is served!

MARIA *finishes her prayer, stands, does her cross one last time, and walks into the dining room.*

MARIA. I am sorry I'm late.

Both she and MARY ANN *take their places at the dining table, they sit, and all begin to eat their porridge.*

Good morning, Mr Evans.

ROBERT. Good morning, Miss Lewis. How did you sleep?

MARIA. Fitfully, I'm afraid.

TWO 55

ROBERT. I am sorry to hear it. What is the reason?

MARIA. I do not know, but my mind was restless.

ROBERT. Perhaps it was the weather. It is very extreme.

MARIA. Indeed.

ROBERT. I stepped outside at dawn, everything is covered. And the winds have brought down part of that old fence at the bottom of the garden, I shall have to mend it, the wood is rotten, I should have done it already. So yes, the wind, and the weight of the snow, did it for me.

Pause, they continue to eat in silence.

You should dress warmly for church, ladies, it will be a freezing walk. Do not forget to cover your faces in scarves, otherwise you will feel the chill, and it will be brutal, mark my words.

MARIA. We shall, Mr Evans.

And again, a pause in the conversation, as they eat their porridge.

ROBERT. The vicar dropped by yesterday, and shared with me the gist of his sermon.

MARY ANN. I know, Father. I let him in.

ROBERT. He was of the idea that as it is the first Sunday of the year, he should strike a note of hope and resolution. No doubt he will have made amendments to it overnight, and brought the present weather into it. Sleeping seeds under the snow, and all that. The man fancies himself a poet.

MARIA. It is a fitting way to start the year. To strike a note of hope, I mean.

MARY ANN. And resolution.

ROBERT. Though I had to advise him against getting carried away. He has a tendency towards sentimentality.

MARIA. He is young.

ROBERT. But his heart is in the right place.

MARIA. That is the most important thing. That we think of others. And that we are not rash.

MARY ANN. Kindness is indeed the most essential virtue, Miss Lewis. Towards others, but also, dare I say it, towards oneself.

ROBERT *can't help raising his eyebrow.*

And as for rashness, Miss Lewis, on that subject too, we are in agreement. One should never do anything, unless it has been considered to the utmost degree.

Pause.

Would you like some more porridge, Father? There is a little in the saucepan.

ROBERT. I have enough here, thank you, Mary Ann.

Pause.

MARY ANN. Father.

ROBERT. Yes, Mary Ann?

But MARIA *jumps in.*

MARIA. Do you think it will last, Mr Evans?

ROBERT. Do I think what will last, Miss Lewis?

MARIA. The snow, I mean.

ROBERT. For the day, at least. But not much longer. The combination of such heavy snowfall and such strong winds is a rare one, we have not seen it for years. By this evening, I am willing to bet that it will start to recede, and then who knows, perhaps tomorrow, the skies will clear and we may even see sunshine.

MARIA. That will be a merciful sight. And beautiful. Blue skies, the sun, and the whole county carpeted in white.

ROBERT. Let's hope for it.

Pause.

MARY ANN. Father.

ROBERT. What is it, Mary Ann?

And again MARIA *jumps in.*

MARIA. When I was a child, I used to love the snow. All children do, do they not? Oh, there are the games, the snowball fights, the sledging and the snowmen and whatnot, and all of that fun to be had. But for me it was something else. For me, it made me feel that everything was going to be alright in the world. I find the sight of the world covered in snow very soothing. I could sit by my window all day staring into the whiteness. It is as if God himself is sending me a sign.

Pause. And, then:

MARY ANN. I will not be coming to church with you today, Father.

ROBERT. You are not feeling well?

MARY ANN. I am in good health, Father.

ROBERT. So, why will you not be coming to church, Mary Ann?

MARY ANN. I shall not be joining you at church today, or on any other Sunday, Father. I am sorry, but I will not be coming to church with you any longer.

ROBERT *has stopped eating, he puts his spoon down.*

ROBERT. Why will you not be coming to church, Mary Ann?

MARY ANN. Because it would be an act of gross hypocrisy for me to do so. To sit by your side, and to kneel, and to pray, and to sing the hymns, and to listen to the sermon, and to bow my head. All of these actions would render me a hypocrite, Father, and I do not wish to be one.

ROBERT. Why would those actions render you a hypocrite, Mary Ann?

MARY ANN. Because I do not believe, any more.

Pause.

I do not believe in the way I used to. It is as if a veil has been lifted from my eyes.

MARIA *starts to stand nervously, she is visibly shaking; she leans for the teapot.*

MARIA. Would you like some more tea, Mr Evans, I can pour you...

MARY ANN *snaps.*

MARY ANN. Please sit, Miss Lewis! The tea can wait. I am not finished talking.

MARIA *sits. The three of them are in silence for a few beats, until* MARY ANN *continues.*

Oh, Father, I believe in the teachings of Christ, the man. I believe in the magnificence and sheer beauty of the story of his life, in the way it invites us to consider our duties towards each other, and the love we should express in action, and the sanctity of justice and equality. I believe in it as allegory and metaphor and as provocation to our better selves. But that is all.

ROBERT. Metaphor?

MARY ANN. Because I do not believe in any of it as indisputable fact, and I certainly do not respect it as dogma. I believe the Gospels are a mixture of historical accuracy and myth, infused with great truth, but interpreted liberally by the men who have written them, and by those who teach them, with the main purpose being to maintain control and shape society in favour, predominantly, of those who hold the reins of economic and social power. It is, for the most part, a perverse misrepresentation of the message of the story. I believe the sublime life of Jesus and the terrible agony of his death, and the radical nature of his teaching, do not deserve to be appropriated by the petty forces of literalism and social conservatism.

Pause.

So you see, I can not stand in that church any more, and pretend any longer. I am sorry, Father.

ROBERT. What are you sorry for?

MARY ANN. For any pain this decision of mine might cause you. The last thing I would ever want is to cause you pain.

A long pause.

ROBERT. And you, Miss Lewis? Will you accompany me to church, this morning?

MARIA. Of course, Mr Evans.

ROBERT. Thank you, Miss Lewis. It is most kind of you.

Pause.

We should leave a little earlier than usual.

He checks the time on his pocket watch.

In five minutes, I think. To give ourselves a little more time. There will be ice on the path, we do not want to slip and break our limbs.

MARIA. Certainly not.

ROBERT. Right. There is something I need to do in my study, if you will excuse me, and then we shall set off.

MARIA. Yes, Mr Evans. I shall help Mary Ann clear the dishes.

ROBERT. Five minutes.

ROBERT *stands and walks out of the room, and into his study.*

MARY ANN *and* MARIA *remain seated, in silence for a few seconds.*

MARIA. He seems to have taken that surprisingly well.

MARY ANN. Then, you do not know my father.

MARY ANN *stands and begins to clear the table;* MARIA *joins her. For the next minute or so, as the two women carry the dishes back into the kitchen,* ROBERT *is in his study, and he is pacing.*

In the kitchen, MARY ANN *places dishes on the sideboard,* MARIA *carries some more in from the dining room.*

Just leave them there, Miss Lewis, I shall wash them all when you and my father are at church.

Then ROBERT *is back, and standing in the door.*

ROBERT. May I speak with you, Mary Ann?

MARY ANN. Of course, Father.

MARIA. I shall go and sit in the parlour room. To give you some privacy.

ROBERT. You can do as you wish, Miss Lewis, but it is not privacy we need in this house this morning, it is something more.

A little confused by his answer, MARIA *nonetheless edges her way out of the room, and makes her way into the parlour room – from where, of course, with the doors open, she can hear just as much. For the next few minutes, as father and daughter remain in the kitchen,* MARIA *hovers in the parlour room, listening to their conversation with increasing curiosity, and distress.*

When ROBERT *speaks, it is as if there is a brewing intensity under the surface, but which he keeps in check.*

Let me ask you something: what do you remember of being a child?

MARY ANN. I do not understand your question, Father.

ROBERT. Do you remember our life at Griff House before your mother died? I would take you with me with the horse and carriage on my morning rounds, this big you were, no taller than my knee, I'd hoist you up into the seat next to mine and we'd ride around the estate from five in the morning, because your mother didn't want you in her way, so off we'd go, your eyes wide open, despite the hour of the day.

MARY ANN. You know I remember.

ROBERT. Do you remember what I would be doing?

MARY ANN. Your job, Father.

ROBERT. Yes, my job. Do you remember what my job was?

MARY ANN. You were estate manager for the Newdigates at Arbury Hall.

ROBERT. Seven thousand acres, yes. But, I mean do you remember what that job entailed?

MARY ANN. Of course I do. I do not understand the nature of your questioning, Father.

ROBERT. Do you remember that flood, in twenty-four I think it was, and that old fool Mallory hadn't prepared his drainage in the right way, and there was that landslide and his farm was as good as written off, and his pigs were drowning in their mess?

MARY ANN. No, Father.

ROBERT. We rode over, and there was nothing but dirt and mud and filth, and you sat in the carriage on a ridge, high up in your little seat, and Mallory was too old to do a thing, both his sons had died within a month of each other the year before, so I was left to carry the animals out of their sty, and down I went into the quagmire, and the muck was up to my chest, and one by one, I lifted them out of it, but they wriggled and fought, and squealed, and fought some more, and I kept slipping in the thick, brown wetness of it all, and falling, and once I thought I was going to die along with the pigs, I was going to drown like them in their excrement, and it must have taken hours but eventually I got them all out, and do you remember what you said, that one of the sows had looked at me with gratitude in her eyes, when I had put her down on the safe grass, above the flooded mess? Do you remember that?

MARY ANN. I don't think so.

ROBERT. With gratitude, you said, and I thought what a thing for a small child to observe.

MARY ANN. I don't remember, Father.

ROBERT. Or do you remember when that vast oak came down only a mile from Arbury Hall, and blocked the track and there was no way round it, so for a week, I had to cut and saw and chop and break, and it was summer, so I'd parked the horse and wagon, with you in it, in the shade of another tree, and you sat there, maybe your mother had given you a slice of bread with jam on it, and I fought that tree from six in the morning till eight in the evening for seven days, until my hands were red, and sore, and splintered, and bleeding? Do you remember that, Mary Ann?

MARY ANN. Yes, I think I do.

ROBERT. And do you remember when your mother died, and we couldn't get the undertakers out, because they said they were overwhelmed, that the Grim Reaper had been busier than ever that summer, so I had to lift her body, which was covered in open sores, out of the bed I'd shared with her for twenty-four years, and wrap it in that sheet, and carry it out of the room, and down the stairs, and into the barn, and rest it there until they could come and collect her?

MARY ANN. Of course, I remember, I nursed her through her final months, and weeks, and days, and hours.

ROBERT. I know you did. And you did so with great care, Mary Ann.

Pause.

We have a contract, you and I. It is not written on paper, but in the earth, and in the seasons.

Pause.

Come with me, I want to show you something.

He turns and walks, with strong purpose, out of the kitchen, and into his study. MARY ANN *has no choice, she follows him.*

In his study, he opens up a drawer in his desk, agitatedly shuffles through some papers, finds the one he is looking for, hands it to her with some force. And his voice and manner are louder now.

What is this? Take it! Tell me what it is.

MARY ANN *takes it from him, scans it, starts to try and make sense of it.*

MARY ANN. I do not know, I have not seen it before, but it looks like a contract.

ROBERT. Yes, that's right, this is a contract too, but this one is in black ink, and the ink has barely dried.

MARY ANN. It is the contract –

ROBERT. For the purchase of this house, that is correct, and look at the price, don't be shy, look at the price, Mary Ann.

MARY ANN. I see it, Father.

ROBERT. It is not a cheap house, is it, Mary Ann?

MARY ANN. I do not know, Father. I have no experience in purchasing houses.

ROBERT. Well, let me tell you then: it is not a cheap house. It is what decades of shovelling your way out of dirt will buy you, and cutting trees down till you think your hands will never feel again, and burying two wives and being left with four starving mouths to feed, and knowing you are the only one to do it. That is the kind of house it is.

MARY ANN. What has the price of Bird Grove to do with it all?

ROBERT. Why did we leave Griff House, Mary Ann?

MARY ANN. Because you gave it to Isaac, so that he could move into it with his wife and take over your job as estate manager.

ROBERT. The boy is up to it. And why did we choose this house and not some small cottage on the estate in which I would be more than happy to spend my final years in peace and quiet?

He opens the drawer again and pulls out a bunch of bills and throws them at her; they land on the floor at her feet. And when he speaks it is now even louder; he is shouting.

Why did we come to Coventry with these outgoings, these bills, these constant demands which are sapping me dry and keeping me up at night? Answer me, Mary Ann, answer me!

MARY ANN. I do not know.

ROBERT. So that we could present to the world a picture of respectability. And what could the reason for that be? My vanity?

MARY ANN. I know the reason.

ROBERT. To find you a home. To find you a husband and a home.

MARY ANN. Well, then you should have forced me to marry Horace Garfield.

ROBERT. It is a good thing I am not a violent man. If I were, this would be the time to strike you. I didn't want that fool anywhere near my precious child!

MARY ANN. Thank heavens for small mercies, then.

ROBERT. To find you a *good* man, and a *good* home. That is the only reason I chose Bird Grove.

Pause.

We have a contract, Mary Ann, but believe me when I say, that you come out of it the better of the two.

Pause.

So go into the hallway, and get your coat and boots on, and don't forget your scarf and gloves, and we shall leave for church in a minute, otherwise we shall be late.

As if mesmerised, this time more effectively than the first, MARY ANN *stands, places the house contract down onto Robert's desk, and slowly steps out of the study, and into the hallway, where she begins to get into her coat and boots, and scarf, and hat.*

She is joined by MARIA, *who steps quietly into the hallway from the parlour room, and joins* MARY ANN *in putting on her coat, and boots, and scarf, and hat. But all along, as she does so, her eyes are fixed on* MARY ANN. MARY ANN *is staring ahead, as if still lost in her father's words.*

ROBERT *takes a few seconds to compose himself; he then picks up all the receipts and bills off the floor, and along with the contract, places them all back into their drawer.*

Once he has done that, he takes a look out the window, at the weather.

Then he too walks into the hallway, and starts to prepare for the walk to the church, by putting on his coat, and scarf, and gloves, and hat.

There's no abating, if anything, it's worse. I was thinking maybe best to take the lower road, down by the Abbots' and past Strawberry Farm. The route is longer, but the path is wider, and will be easier, and there is the fence on each side should we need it for balance. There will be ice on the ground, and if we go the usual way, it will be worse, because the ridge is so exposed, with nothing to hold on to.

They are all nearly finished with their dressing. Then, slowly, MARY ANN *begins to reverse the process. She slowly takes off her scarf, hangs it up, then her gloves, then her hat, then her coat.* MARIA *watches her with incremental dread;* ROBERT *watches too, but he does not look as surprised.*

Finally, MARY ANN *slowly walks into the parlour room.* ROBERT *follows her,* MARIA *remains in the hallway.*

There is a long pause before she eventually speaks.

MARY ANN. I shall not be coming to church, Father. If nothing else, you have emboldened my doubts, and confirmed my suspicions. It seems neither of us go to church for solace or salvation. I go there only to keep you happy, you go there as if you go to market.

ROBERT *explodes, his voice shatters the quiet of the house.*

ROBERT. DOUBT YOUR OWN FAITH, YOUNG LADY, BUT DO NOT DOUBT MINE!

Pause.

MARY ANN. I shall be here when you return.

ROBERT *heads back into the hallway.*

ROBERT. Let us go, Miss Lewis, otherwise we shall be late.

ROBERT *walks stridently to the front door, and opens it. MARIA steps out of the house, and he follows her, closing the door behind him.*

For a few seconds, MARY ANN *just stands in the parlour room, staring ahead.*

Then the front door opens, and ROBERT *storms back into the house, and into the parlour room. His coat and hair are specked with snow.*

Then you are to leave this house. I shall sell it, and move to a small cottage on the estate, as was my original plan. You are free to do what you like. You could be a governess, though I can't imagine most parents will want you anywhere near their children, with these ideas you have in your head. But you are to stay with me no longer. I will not be humiliated. We will leave Bird Grove, and go our separate ways.

He is about to go, and then hovers for a minute, before he continues. When he speaks he chooses his words carefully, and it is as if he is about to break.

And one more thing. If we do not believe together, Mary Ann, if we do not pray together, if we do not agree on what it is that makes life meaningful, and good, and precious, then what will become of us? We will be like a thousand scattered leaves raging in that storm outside. Like a Tower of Babel. Like a madhouse full of madmen and madwomen, tearing each other apart.

Pause.

On your head be it.

And he leaves the house.

MARY ANN *does not move for a few seconds.*

Then, slowly, she starts to do so but it looks as if she might collapse, and fall to the floor; her steps are unsteady.

She starts gasping for breath, overcome with emotion. Slowly, with difficulty, she starts to walk out of the parlour room, into the hallway, and then, leaning from time to time against the furniture, and against the walls, for support, she makes her way into Robert's study, and towards his desk.

When she reaches it, she opens the drawer with the contracts and bills in it, and brings them all out, spreads them out onto the desktop, until she finds the one she is looking for: the contract for the purchase of Bird Grove. She picks it up in her hands, which are trembling.

MARY ANN. I did not sign it, I was not there, I do not want it!

Holding the contract in her hands, she stumbles towards the window, as if she cannot breathe, as if it will save her, as if it is her only way out of the house.

When she reaches it, she unlocks it, and with difficulty, opens it.

When the window is open wide, the full force of the blizzard is loud, and violent, and overwhelming. It is as if the weather, as if nature herself, is feeling MARY ANN's *despair.*

I will be heard! I will be heard!

She holds the contract high above her head, and tears it into many pieces.

The weather enters the house, and becomes one with MARY ANN.

It scatters the pieces of the contract, like confetti, across the room.

Blackout.

Interval.

THREE

It is a morning, three months later, April, 1842.

It is fine spring weather, rays of sunshine make their way through the windows, and into the house.

ROBERT *is in his study, reading the local journal. He looks more dishevelled than when we last saw him, and strangely older.*

The room looks messy, as if it has been left uncared for. Piles of papers everywhere, a few stray books, a decanter or two standing on random surfaces.

ROBERT *slowly rests the paper on his knee, and stares ahead, lost in what looks like unhappy thought.*

There is a knock and MARIA *walks into the room, with a bucket and mop.* ROBERT *immediately returns to his journal, and pretends to be reading.*

MARIA. I am finished with the kitchen, Mr Evans, so all the rooms have been done now, apart from your study. And your clothes have all been laundered and ironed and I have put them away in your cupboard.

ROBERT. You are too kind, Miss Lewis.

  MARIA *places the bucket and mop down on the floor, walks up to* ROBERT*'s desk, on which many papers are strewn.*

MARIA. I'd like to clear all these papers away, sir, but I do not want to muddle things.

ROBERT. Just make a pile of them, if you will, and I shall sort them out later. Let us at least attempt to create an illusion of order, if not the thing itself.

  So, she starts to gather all the scattered papers and begins to make a neat pile of them.

MARIA. I bumped into Mrs Begg from down the road when I went for my walk this morning, she was concerned about you. She is a lovely lady. She mentioned that there is a young girl she knows who could easily drop in and clean the house for you three times a week. It would make things easier, would it not?

ROBERT. Mrs Begg is not a lovely lady, Miss Lewis, and she is not concerned. She is a nosy old harridan, and would like nothing more than to know what has been happening within these walls. And I am not willing to have one of her agents snooping around the place, like a rat. I will manage just fine on my own, thank you.

MARIA. As you wish, sir.

MARIA has finished at the desk; she walks over to the bucket and mop, picks them up, and heads over to the window, to start mopping from the edge of the room.

I shall give the floors a quick mop, sir, and then I'll be out from under your feet.

ROBERT. Thank you, Miss Lewis.

The sound of a horse and carriage approaching; MARIA *looks out.*

MARIA. Oh, there is a carriage.

ROBERT. I am not expecting anyone.

MARIA. Yes, it is pulling up in front of the house. Someone is here to see you, Mr Evans.

ROBERT. I do not want visitors this morning!

The faint sound of a carriage door opening, and closing, as somebody steps out of the carriage.

MARIA. Oh, dear me.

ROBERT. Who is it, Miss Lewis?

MARIA. It is the Brays, Mr Evans.

ROBERT. The Brays!

MARIA. Yes, it is Mr and Mrs Bray. They are looking very purposeful.

ROBERT. They always are.

He stands with difficulty, drops his journal to the floor.

MARIA. Both of them have stepped out of the carriage.

ROBERT. I would rather Attila the Hun were visiting!

MARIA. Oh, she has seen me, Mrs Bray has seen me.

ROBERT. Well, of course she has, you are standing by the window, Miss Lewis, like a lamp post!

MARIA. She is waving.

MARIA *waves back*.

ROBERT. Miss Lewis, what are you doing, waving back at them? I tell you, I do not want to see the Brays!

MARIA. Oh, they are stepping towards the house.

ROBERT. It is damned uncivil of them to drop in like this. And I will not see them!

MARIA *stares at him; they are now both in a panic*.

MARIA. What shall we do, Mr Evans?

ROBERT. How dare they show up, uninvited?!

And then, the cheerful sound of the doorbell.

Do not open the door. We shall pretend we are not in.

MARIA. But they just saw me.

ROBERT. Yes, because you were hovering by the window, Miss Lewis.

MARIA. Mrs Bray waved.

ROBERT. And you waved back, I know, I saw. This is most inconvenient!

More ringing from the door.

MARIA. Oh, Mr Evans, what shall we do?

ROBERT. Well, you have left us no choice, you must open the door. But you are to tell them that I am not in.

MARIA. But you are, Mr Evans.

ROBERT. Yes, I know that, Miss Lewis, I am not a lunatic, I know I am standing here talking to you, but you are to tell them that I am not!

MARIA. Oh, Mr Evans, I have never lied in my entire life, I do not want to break the habit, and besides, I am certain I would not be very good at it.

ROBERT. Well then, tell them I am busy, very, very, busy.

MARIA. Doing what, Mr Evans? They know you are retired.

And more insistent bell-ringing from the front door.

ROBERT. Oh, for goodness' sake, Miss Lewis, make something up, I don't know, tell them I have taken up Latin, the violin, or watercolours. But I will not see the Brays!

MARIA. As you wish.

MARIA *makes her way nervously towards the door, and the hallway.*

ROBERT. They can talk the Pope out of Catholicism, I will not see them!

MARIA *steps out of the room, closing the door behind her. She crosses the hallway and opens the front door.* CHARLES *and* CARA *step into the house.*

(*For the next few moments, as* MARIA *and the* BRAYS *are chatting,* ROBERT *is desperately running around his study, as if looking for somewhere to hide. He tries standing behind the curtains, but realises his feet stick out, he then considers concealing himself under his desk, but it is too tight a space. Finally, he tries squeezing into a cupboard but that too is too small for him.*

Eventually, he realises the absurdity of his actions, and stops, before opening the door, and facing his unwelcome guests.)

CARA. Miss Lewis, how lovely to see you, we were not expecting to find you here!

MARIA. Good morning, Mrs Bray, Mr Bray.

CHARLES. Good morning, Miss Lewis!

CARA. But what brings you to Bird Grove, my dear?

MARIA. I am merely visiting for a couple of days, Mrs Bray, just in order to help Mr Evans with a few jobs around the house.

CARA. Ah, yes, they are not very good on their own, are they?

CHARLES. Hopeless.

CARA. Everything falls apart. I am sure Mr Evans must be very grateful to have you around.

CHARLES. And he is in, is he?

MARIA. Who?

CHARLES. Mr Evans, of course.

MARIA. Mr Evans?

CARA. Yes, my dear, Mr Evans. Is he in?

MARIA. No. I mean, yes, of course he is in, but not in this room.

CARA. We can see that, Miss Lewis.

MARIA. He cannot see you, I'm afraid, because he is very, very busy.

CARA. Busy, doing what?

MARIA. Watercolours.

Pause. MARIA *is frozen.*

And Latin. Watercolours and Latin.

CHARLES. Simultaneously? How novel.

MARIA. And he is learning the violin.

The study door opens, and ROBERT *steps out.*

ROBERT. It is alright, Miss Lewis. Good morning.

CHARLES. Oh, Mr Evans, how lovely it is to see you on this glorious spring day.

CARA. We have missed you, Mr Evans, we hope you don't mind us calling on you.

ROBERT. It is not conventional to drop in, like this, without a warning.

Pause.

MARIA. If you'll excuse me, I shall continue with my chores. I was about to mop the floor in Mr Evans' study.

MARIA *scuttles off into the study, closing the door behind her. But she does not immediately reach for the bucket and mop, instead she hovers by the door to try and listen in on the conversation in the hallway.*

There is a short, awkward pause before CARA *speaks.*

CARA. The honest truth is, Mr Evans, that we felt – perhaps instinctively – that an invitation to Bird Grove was not imminent, and that if we had attempted to elicit one from you, we would not have been successful.

ROBERT. And so you hurl yourselves at me, instead.

Pause.

To what do I owe the pleasure of your visit?

CHARLES. It is not a pleasure for you, Mr Evans, so you need not feign that it is. Let us be honest with each other. Honesty, I think, is useful, when the conversation called for is of an essential, and grave nature.

ROBERT. I am not prepared for such a conversation, Mr Bray, and I do not wish to have it with you. Is that honest enough?

CHARLES. Emphatically. But I nevertheless beseech you for a few moments of your time, so that I can please try and change your mind and prove to you why such a conversation is long overdue, and must now occur.

ROBERT. Let us have it then.

CHARLES. But, it is not a conversation for the hallway. May we step into your study, please?

In the study, MARIA *makes a dash away from the door and to the bucket and mop.*

ROBERT *stalls, undecided.*

Then, reluctantly, he opens the study door and makes a gesture for CHARLES *and* CARA *to enter the room. They do so, and he follows, closing the door behind him.* MARIA *is flustered.*

MARIA. Maybe I should leave this for another time, I shall go peel those potatoes for your tea, Mr Evans.

ROBERT. We shall not be changing our plans for Mr and Mrs Bray. So, you shall remain in this room, and finish your job, Miss Lewis.

MARIA. Yes, Mr Evans.

ROBERT *goes and sits behind his desk. He does not offer the* BRAYS *a seat, so they remain standing.*

For the entire scene, MARIA *is quietly mopping the floor of the room, around them.*

ROBERT. To what, then, do I owe the *inconvenience* of your visit?

Pause.

CHARLES. It has been three months –

CARA. Three months and two days.

CHARLES. Three months and two days, since you... since it was decided that Mary Ann should leave Bird Grove and reside with her brother and sister-in-law at Griff House.

THREE   75

ROBERT. I know how long it's been.

CHARLES. And so, we come to you, as friends, and hopeful arbitrators, to help negotiate a peace.

ROBERT. But you have not been invited, sir, to take on the role.

CHARLES. We have, by one of the parties.

ROBERT. But not the other. That is not a promising start to any process of arbitration.

Pause.

CARA. Perhaps then, it is best to start by what is most obvious, or at least ought to be. But maybe there is merit in declaring it, all the same.

ROBERT. And what is that?

CARA. That Mary Ann loves you, sir, in the most profound and genuine way.

ROBERT. She has a funny way of showing it.

CARA. It is sad that you feel that. Maybe, what is at question then, is less the degree of love that she has for you, or the quality of it, but more the meaning of the word itself. Love is not blind obedience, sir, that is something altogether different.

ROBERT. I shall propose, Mrs Bray, a different beginning for our conversation. One that I think more apt. Besides, to enter a discussion on the meaning of love is one, no doubt, in which you would excel, and I would falter. You are better with words than I am, or at least more persuasive in your arguments. So, that would not be fair. I will plead for simplicity.

CHARLES. What is your beginning then, Mr Evans?

ROBERT. My beginning, as a father, is to ask when did all this start? When did my dear daughter's mind, her heart, her life, take the direction which has brought us now to this sad stalemate we are at, and to the total breakdown of our relationship.

CHARLES. It is a fair beginning.

ROBERT. And I would venture to suggest that it started on the day she met the two of you, and visited Rosehill.

CARA. You flatter us, Mr Evans. Your daughter would find new ways of looking at the world if she had to dig them out of the earth with her own bare hands.

CHARLES. She is a remarkable human being, Mr Evans.

MARIA. That, she is.

The front door opens, and MARY ANN *walks into the house. She slowly starts to take off her bonnet and coat, and hangs them up in the hallway.*

Then, for the next few moments, as the conversation continues in the study, MARY ANN *starts to walk around the other rooms, as if reacquainting herself with them. She softly steps from the hallway into the kitchen, then into the dining room, finally into the parlour room.*

CHARLES. We spoke that evening, a few days before Christmas, half in seriousness, half in jest, on the merits and pitfalls of both progress and tradition, did we not? And we agreed, Mr Evans, that there is a thin line between the two which needs to be walked upon with care, and caution. That sometimes, tradition can shackle and bind us, but that progress, in turn, can overwhelm and daunt. We are living, are we not, in times of great change.

ROBERT. That, I will concede.

CHARLES. Oh, I am not referring to the advancements in industries, and machinery, and whether we will be able to travel by train from Birmingham to London in seven hours, or four, or two. These are trivialities. No, sir, I am talking of another type of progress. That of the human mind and spirit.

CARA. That sort of progress should not be hindered, Mr Evans. In fact, it is the duty of every civilised society to encourage the potential of any harbingers of that progress, whoever they may be.

CHARLES. From the first day we met Mary Ann, Mr Evans, both Cara and I have had an unshakeable faith and confidence in your daughter's potential. Her thirst for knowledge, her infinite curiosity, and her unquenchable desire to find answers to the most burning questions of existence, will assure her of a shining, brilliant future.

CARA. And above all, there is her gift for writing. Oh, she is still searching for her voice, Mr Evans, she flounders and flaps her wings, and falls, and lifts herself up again, but the talent, sir, is vast and unmistakable.

ROBERT. You are intelligent people, and astute. At least in spotting my daughter's genius. But how astounding that you have not entertained the notion that I have spotted it myself. I know the girl a little better than you do.

CHARLES. Of course.

ROBERT. But I am a father, and I am old. I am not interested in the world's improvement, in its glorious strides towards further enlightenment, towards what you term 'progress', Mr and Mrs Bray.

Pause.

Did it ever occur to you, even for a second, that a father's main duty is to protect his child from harm, and scorn, and ostracisation? To turn her back on the church, and on its teachings, would ensure that she would know all three.

Pause.

So, you see, it is not only myself that I am thinking of.

The door slowly opens, MARY ANN *steps into the room.*

ROBERT *freezes; father and daughter stare at each other from a few feet apart.*

MARY ANN. I have left my case in the carriage. But I could not wait outside. And besides, Cara, Charles, I can not expect you to speak for me.

MARIA. Oh, my dear girl.

MARY ANN. Good morning, Miss Lewis.

ROBERT. I am ambushed, then. Outnumbered.

CARA. It is not a battle, sir.

MARY ANN. Hello, Father.

ROBERT. Why have you come here today, Mary Ann?

MARY ANN. To talk to you.

ROBERT. There is nothing much to say. Nothing has changed.

MARY ANN. This is my home. The only one I have.

ROBERT. And you may return to it. The door is always open to you.

CHARLES. Of course it is.

MARY ANN. Thank you.

ROBERT. As long as you agree once more to join me at church.

MARY ANN. We must find a way of moving forward, Father.

ROBERT. I am intransigent.

Pause.

If you do not accept that one condition, there is no point in your being here, Mary Ann.

MARY ANN. So you would have me homeless.

ROBERT. That is your choice.

MARY ANN. My choice is to live truthfully, Father. I am sorry that we do not share agreement at this moment on what the truth is. But you cannot force me to live by your definition of it, if it does not chime with mine.

ROBERT. Oh, so the truth is not something we all share, then. How novel. You have yours, and I have mine, and Miss Lewis has hers, and the Brays most definitely have one of their own, or probably one each. The truth then is like a piece of clothing, is it, or a bauble. Each has his own. What a world you propose, Mary Ann.

MARY ANN. I did not say we do not share a common truth, Father, I suggested the difference is in our definitions. Or simply, our perspectives of it.

Pause.

And anyway, maybe that truth is ever-shifting. Maybe it is not carved in stone, or even written on paper. Maybe it changes with our understanding.

Pause.

Cara, Charles, Miss Lewis, may I ask you all a favour?

CARA. Anything.

MARY ANN. Could you please leave me alone with my father, for a few minutes?

CARA. Is it not best we stay? I mean, to help you reach an agreement.

MARY ANN. It is not necessary.

CHARLES. Of course, Mary Ann. We shall wait next door.

MARY ANN. Thank you.

MARIA. I shall finish up in the kitchen.

MARY ANN. Thank you, Miss Lewis.

MARIA leaves the room, with the bucket and mop, and makes her way to the kitchen. She is followed out of the study by CHARLES and CARA. But CARA pauses at the door.

CARA. But may I speak to you, please, for just one moment, Mary Ann?

MARY ANN. Of course. I shall return, Father.

MARY ANN follows CARA and CHARLES out of the room. MARY ANN closes the door behind her; CARA leads her into the parlour room, CHARLES follows them.

As they speak, ROBERT *remains in his study, pours himself a drink.*

In the parlour room, the BRAYS *speak quietly so that they will not be heard.*

CARA. Mary Ann.

MARY ANN. Cara.

CARA. I understand that you need to make peace with your father.

CHARLES. And that you need to return to your home.

CARA. It is your decision to make. But, my dear girl, tread carefully.

Pause.

You should not – you *cannot* – go back to how things were, my darling.

CHARLES. It would be a betrayal.

CARA. You have taken a heroic stand. A stand against hypocrisy, indoctrination, the arrogance of dogma.

CHARLES. To backtrack now would be calamitous, my dear.

CARA. You cannot do it.

MARIA *has just arrived from the kitchen; she is in the doorway.*

MARIA. Your father loves you, Mary Ann.

CHARLES. If Isaac will not have you at Griff House, you can come to Rosehill.

MARIA. He worships and adores you.

CARA. There is always a room for you there.

CHARLES. But you should stand by what you believe in.

CARA. It is imperative. It will define you.

Pause.

MARY ANN. You are such dear friends. All three of you. Thank you.

Pause.

You are right, Cara. It is my decision to make. Can I ask you to wait here?

She steps out of the parlour room, into the hallway. For a few seconds, she hovers outside the door to Robert's study. Then, when she is ready, she gently knocks, and enters.

ROBERT *is sitting in his armchair again, drink in hand.*

MARY ANN *starts to walk around the room, taking it all in again.*

You have allowed this room to become messy, Father.

ROBERT. Miss Lewis was tidying it, when you surprised us. She piled up all the paperwork.

MARY ANN walks up to the desk, and starts looking through the pile of papers.

MARY ANN. Bills, bills, bills.

She picks one up, looks at it.

Who is Mr Wilkes?

ROBERT. He does odd jobs in the garden. I could not manage it myself any more, and the ivy got out of hand, so he came to trim it before eyebrows were raised.

And now she looks at another.

MARY ANN. And Henry Briggs and Son?

ROBERT. The chimney sweepers.

MARY ANN. Of course. They are not cheap.

She puts down the bills.

We do not need to stay in this house.

Pause.

You implied that the reason we moved to Bird Grove was to help find me a husband, and a home.

ROBERT. One of the reasons.

MARY ANN. The main reason, I'm sure. So, I would be happy for you to sell Bird Grove, and we move to a small cottage where life will be cheaper. If nothing else, Father, it places a great deal of pressure on me.

ROBERT. But I have come to love this house. And I have worked hard all my life for it.

MARY ANN. I understand. Bird Grove announces to the world your achievements and position in it. That is important to you.

Again, she starts to move around the room, stopping every so often to pick something up, put it in the right place.

How is your back?

ROBERT. Not much change. When I rise from bed in the morning, I feel as if I will not be able to stand on my own two legs.

MARY ANN. But you do.

ROBERT. Eventually.

She looks at him in his chair.

MARY ANN. You do not look comfortable in your chair.

ROBERT. That is because I am not.

She walks up to him, reaches out for his hand.

MARY ANN. Stand up, please.

He does as he's told.

Well, no wonder you are not comfortable, you only have the one cushion. I thought we decided you need at least two, for support. Wait.

She moves over to another chair, takes a cushion from it, props it up behind him on his armchair.

That should be better, now. Sit back.

He does as he's told, sits down again.

How is that?

ROBERT. It is better.

MARY ANN. Of course it is. You should always have both cushions. Your back needs all the help it can get.

ROBERT. It certainly does. I am an old horse.

MARY ANN. Well, that's an improvement, anyway.

Now she drifts over to the window, looks out.

ROBERT. Isaac and Sarah have been treating you well, at Griff House?

MARY ANN. Sarah has been kind, yes. Isaac has tolerated me.

ROBERT. He is a busy man, Mary Ann.

MARY ANN. I have been reading a lot.

ROBERT. Geology?

MARY ANN. No, I have exhausted the subject. Fiction, mostly.

ROBERT. Stories, then.

MARY ANN. Yes, stories.

Pause.

The magnolia is magnificent this year.

ROBERT. This is the time for it. It doesn't last long, but it is a thing of great beauty.

MARY ANN. This April has been very kind to us, has it not? Hardly any rain, and these blue, blue skies.

Pause.

I know this country and I know its people, and I know this community. And I know how your presence at Trinity Church, without my attendance by your side, will have prompted comment, and sneer, and yes, downright gossip.

All of these are to be expected, unfortunately. And I also know something about men, because I have lived with you and my brothers, and about how there is nothing more bitter to you, than shame in the eyes of others. You have built prisons for us all out of that shame.

She walks until she is a few feet away from him, and stands facing him.

I shall come to church with you, Father.

ROBERT. I am glad to hear it.

MARY ANN. But not the morning service. Never communion. Only matins.

ROBERT. Only matins, then.

MARY ANN. I shall not pray, Father, so do not ever ask me to do so, and I shall not kneel, and I shall not sing the hymns. Discreetly, I will abstain. But I shall accompany you there every Sunday, and stand by your side when you greet the congregation, and then sit by your side in the pews.

ROBERT. Yes.

MARY ANN. That is now our bond, Father, and I will ask you to please respect it. If once you ask me to kneel, or pray, or sing, I shall leave the church, and I shall leave Bird Grove, and I shall never return. But if you do not, I will be there by your side, as I have been my entire life.

ROBERT. I shall not ask you, then.

Pause.

This is all good. You can go and fetch your bag from the carriage, and you can ask the Brays to leave, we shall not be needing them any more. Miss Lewis has tidied your bedroom, it is ready for you.

MARY ANN. No, Father. Not yet. I have not finished.

Pause.

There is something I would like to read you.

Pause. She brings a folded sheet of paper out of her pocket, unfolds it.

It is a few lines I wrote you when I was at Griff House. I took myself on a walk one morning, and found a spot by the canal, and sat myself down, and wrote you a letter which I never sent. This is a part of it.

She reads.

'You have loved me, Father, and you continue to love me, I am sure of it. But you love me in a way that subjugates my needs, my thoughts, and my desires. You love me as long as I do not challenge you, or question you, or demand you to hear me. I do not know what sort of love that is, but I know it is not the way I have loved, and continue to love you.'

She puts the letter back in her pocket, looks across the room at ROBERT.

So, what I ask from you today, is that you interrogate in earnest that way in which you love me, and ask yourself if it is worthy of either of us. Will you do that for me, Father?

ROBERT. It depends, Mary Ann.

Her tone changes, it becomes steelier.

MARY ANN. No, Father, it depends on nothing at all. Not any more. My demand is unconditional.

ROBERT. Unconditional.

MARY ANN. Yes, unconditional. I demand you, Father, to undertake that interrogation with all the gravity you can bring to it, and I need your word that you will do so. Otherwise, there is no point in me returning here today, and there is no point in furthering this conversation. The Brays have offered me a home, and I shall take up their offer, if you cannot give me that, at least.

ROBERT. I shall consider the way in which I love you, then.

Pause.

You have my word.

MARY ANN. Thank you.

Pause.

So you will not sell Bird Grove?

ROBERT. Not now. Not any more.

MARY ANN. I don't suspect, you see, that I shall ever marry, or if I ever do, it will not be for a very long time. I want to read, and read, and read, and Father, I want to *write*. There are so many things I want to say, from my heart and from my soul, and my only prayer is that I am given enough time to do that writing.

ROBERT. God will grant you that, I am sure of it.

MARY ANN. So, yes, Father, I suspect that I shall be here with you, by your side, in this house, and I shall nurse you, and I shall be holding your hand when it is your time to leave this troubled life.

She walks towards the door, but stops and turns before she reaches it.

Of course I remember you hoisting me up into that carriage, and taking me to your work, and I remember that fallen oak tree, and I remember when you carried dear Mother's body down the stairs after I had nursed her through her final days. We were there together, weren't we, you and I.

ROBERT. We were.

MARY ANN opens the door, leaves the room, closes it behind her.

She walks into the parlour room, where MARIA, CHARLES *and* CARA *are waiting for her.*

MARY ANN. I am staying.

MARIA, with joy and relief, puts her arms around MARY ANN, *and embraces her.* CARA *and* CHARLES *throw each other a quick look of concern.*

In his study, ROBERT *lifts himself out of his armchair with some difficulty, and makes his way towards his desk. When he reaches it, he leans gently against it, and lowers his head.*

He weeps, quietly at first, not wanting to be heard.

Then, his whole body stoops over, and he begins to sob, and his shoulders heave.

He cries like a man who has never cried before.

The lights fade to black.

FOUR

It is seven years later, August, 1849.

It is a warm summer evening, the windows are all open, and the house is glowing in the slow, dying light of the day.

In the middle of Robert's study, there is a large, open trunk, filled with books.

MARY ANN *is kneeling by that trunk, carefully placing the last remaining books into it, one by one. As she does so, she holds each book carefully, sometimes leafing through it, before placing it into the trunk.*

There is now a made bed that sits in the middle of the room.

MARIA *is sitting in the parlour room, she is knitting.*

In the middle of the hallway, there is a medium-sized trunk.

CARA *comes down the steps, carrying a third, smaller trunk. She places it down by the other one, then steps into the study.*

CARA. I have brought the smaller trunk downstairs. The one with the warmer clothes, for Switzerland.

MARY ANN. It was not your task, Cara, to carry that trunk down, I told you I was going to do it myself.

CARA. From tomorrow we are fellow travellers, we might as well get used to carrying each other's luggage.

MARY ANN *puts the last of the books into the trunk, and closes it.*

MARY ANN. I do hope these books make it to Switzerland before we do. I am told there is little to do in Geneva but gawp at the Alps.

CARA. Do not worry, Charles will make sure you are not bookless. His books and yours will both be waiting for us when we arrive at the pension, and then you can spend your days buried in them, I shall do the gawping.

The front door opens, and ISAAC *walks into the house with* MR BARING, *an elderly solicitor, appropriately suited, and carrying a leather briefcase.* ISAAC *sticks his head in the study door.*

ISAAC. Ah, there you are, good evening, Mary Ann.

MARY ANN. Isaac, at last! I thought you were never coming.

MARY ANN *shows the two men into the study;* CARA *hovers.*

BARING. It is my fault, Miss Evans, we had a situation at the office, with a client who was most obstructive, and ignorant of timekeeping.

ISAAC. You remember Mr Hugo Baring, Father's solicitor.

MARY ANN. Of course I do.

BARING. I daresay, I have had more to do with your sister over the years, than I have done with you, Mr Evans, especially during your father's long illness.

MARY ANN. And this is my friend, Mrs Bray.

BARING. *The* Mrs Bray? Of Rosehill?

CARA. I believe so.

BARING. How satisfying to put a face to the name.

CARA. I hope it lives up to the expectation.

An embarrassed chuckle from BARING.

ISAAC. So, you are all off to the Continent in the morning.

CARA. My husband and I are kidnapping your sister, it is true.

ISAAC. I thought you did that years ago, Mrs Bray.

BARING. France?

CARA. Two weeks in Paris, three in Italy, and then, October in Geneva. Charles and I will be back in the first week of November.

MARY ANN. I may stay longer. For I am not yet sure what I shall be returning to.

She looks at ISAAC, *who immediately tenses up.*

Which brings us to the business, at hand. We should proceed. If nothing else, I'm sure you have a home to get to, Mr Baring.

BARING. Indeed. I do believe my wife has made chicken pie this evening.

MARY ANN. Well, we don't want to keep either of them waiting!

CARA. I shall be next door.

MARY ANN. Thank you, Cara.

She leads her to the door; CARA *leaves the room and joins* MARIA *in the parlour room.* MARY ANN *is then about to close the study door, but decides against it, and purposefully leaves it ajar.*

CARA *sits down on the sofa in the parlour room, opposite* MARIA, *who is still knitting. The two women remain silent for the whole scene, with their ears tuned in to the conversation which is emerging from the study; they can hear the greater part of it.*

In the study, MARY ANN *is leading* BARING *towards the desk and chairs but there is the bed in the middle of the room, which they have to negotiate.*

Forgive the bed, Mr Baring, we moved my father down here for the last few months of his life, and I have not yet had a chance to remove it.

BARING. Ah, yes, of course, in fact he was in here, when I came the last time, and we discussed all the details… of what we are about to discuss!

MARY ANN. It suited him well. On the sunnier days, I could help him down into the garden for a little fresh air, and to be surrounded by the trees and flowers he loved so much.

BARING. Nature is a balm in illness.

MARY ANN *indicates one of the chairs*.

MARY ANN. Please, sit.

He does so. ISAAC *goes and takes his father's chair, behind the desk, so* MARY ANN *has to sit in the only remaining one; she does so.* BARING *places his briefcase on his knees and starts to rummage through it, looking for something.*

BARING. Your father was a beloved client of mine.

ISAAC. He held you in high esteem.

BARING. And to sit here, in this beautiful room, surrounded by the things I am sure he loved so much, is a fitting way for me to bid him farewell, and a tribute to all his achievements.

MARY ANN. Thank you for your generous words, Mr Baring, I am sure he would have appreciated them.

BARING. He was a man of character. No doubt the loss will mark you.

MARY ANN. His absence is certainly felt.

BARING. I am sure of it.

Pause. He brings out from his briefcase a couple of documents.

So, for the business at hand.

MARY ANN. Yes.

BARING. As you know already, Miss Evans, your brother Isaac is the executor of your father's will and is under no legal obligation to share with you the details therein, apart from the components which directly involve yourself, as a listed beneficiary.

MARY ANN. Well, that is convenient, because they are the only parts I am interested in.

They look at her.

Oh, I do not mean to be disrespectful, but of course my main priority, at the beginning of this rather overwhelming new chapter of my life, is to know how I will survive, and continue.

BARING. Of course.

MARY ANN. So, I am not expecting you to go with a comb through every detail of my father's testament, Mr Baring, only the sections which will make clear to me how I am about to proceed with the challenging business of living my life as an unmarried woman.

ISAAC. That is your choice, Mary Ann.

MARY ANN. For now, it is.

BARING. Of course, Miss Evans. But I was going to continue and say, that your brother has made it clear, that despite the lack of legal compulsion, he is more than happy to share those details with you, and following his generous lead, I have taken the liberty of making you a copy of the entire will and testament, should you wish to peruse it at any time, either during our conversation this evening, or after it is completed.

ISAAC. It is best to be open.

BARING *hands one of the documents to* MARY ANN, *keeps one for himself.*

MARY ANN. Thank you.

BARING. But since you have been clear on the matter, I shall of course skip the formalities, and draw our focus exclusively to the clauses in the document which directly concern yourself.

MARY ANN. Thank you, Mr Baring.

BARING *looks down at the will, starts to flick through it.*

BARING. So, then I shall draw your attention, in fact, to the one singular clause in which you are named as beneficiary, and that is clause six-point-two on page three.

She starts to look for it in her copy.

Do you see it, Miss Evans?

She finds it.

MARY ANN. I do.

BARING. I shall read it aloud, for Mr Evans' benefit, even though, as executor, he has been made acquainted with it, already.

He reads from his copy.

'To my daughter, Mary Ann Evans, I hereby bequest the total sum of two thousand pounds in trust, to be paid to her on a six-monthly regular basis over the ten consecutive years following my passing, and a gift of one hundred pounds in cash to be handed over to her immediately, once the sum becomes available following probate.'

BARING *looks up, at* MARY ANN.

And that is it.

Pause.

MARY ANN. And Bird Grove, if I may ask?

BARING *throws* ISAAC *a look, almost as if he is asking for permission to answer. He then turns over to the previous page of the will, and scans it.*

BARING. Your father's various properties, in both the Warwickshire area, and in Derbyshire, have been shared equally between his two sons, that being, Mr Isaac Evans, seated to my left, and your father's eldest son, also Robert Evans, from his first wife, Mrs Harriet Evans, née Poynton. It is a clean split – all the Derbyshire property is inherited by Mr Robert Evans, all the property in the Warwickshire area by your brother, Mr Isaac Evans.

MARY ANN. Including Bird Grove.

BARING. Yes, including Bird Grove.

Pause.

Your father had sons, Miss Evans. It is the way of the world.

Across the hallway, in the parlour room, CARA *has heard every word.*

CARA. The wicked way of the world.

BARING. Is there anything else, Miss Evans? Any questions, queries, clarifications you need?

MARY ANN. Yes, there is one more thing.

BARING. What is it?

MARY ANN. His collection of books.

ISAAC squirms in his seat.

They are not hugely valuable, I mean monetarily, but they were much loved by him, and prized possessions. We spent many an evening in this very room, towards the end of his life, with me reading *Ivanhoe* to him. So there is a sentimental connection, you understand.

BARING. Of course.

MARY ANN *then turns and points to one of the bookshelves.*

MARY ANN. In fact, they are there now, on those shelves, all of them, apart from the ones I have packed to take to Europe with me.

Again BARING *throws* ISAAC *a quick look, as if to check with him whether he should proceed.*

BARING. They are indeed listed in your father's will but I thought you'd asked –

MARY ANN. We will make the exception. Please.

Again, BARING *starts to leaf through his copy of the will until he finds what he's looking for.*

BARING. I shall therefore draw your attention to clause sixteen-point-three on page seven of the document, under the heading *Miscellaneous*.

And he reads.

'To my eldest daughter… Fanny Evans, I bequest my entire collection of books, which have brought me so much pleasure during my life, with the sole request that they shall be looked after by her during her lifetime.'

MARY ANN. But Fanny isn't even a reader.

ISAAC. Fanny has children, the books shall pass on to her boys.

BARING *closes the document. There is a pause.*

MARY ANN. How strange.

Pause.

He is punishing me.

BARING. I beg your pardon?

MARY ANN. Forgive me, I am thinking aloud.

She suddenly stands, and walks over to the desk, reaches for a pencil and a piece of paper. She seems distracted, at a loss.

I will have to do the arithmetic, if you'll excuse me. What is the amount did you say that I have been left in trust?

BARING *is about to return to the document, but* ISAAC *answers before he gets the chance.*

ISAAC. Two thousand pounds.

BARING. That is correct.

She is doing the sums.

MARY ANN. To be paid to me every six months, is that correct?

ISAAC. Indeed.

MARY ANN. So that comes to…

ISAAC. A hundred pounds, every six months, Mary Ann.

MARY ANN. Which comes to a monthly sum of –

ISAAC. Sixteen pounds.

MARY ANN. Thank you, Isaac. Isaac is the mathematician in our family.

BARING. I can see that.

MARY ANN *returns to her chair, and almost falls into it.*

MARY ANN. That is not enough to live on. Not nearly enough.

An awkward pause.

BARING. Is there anything else, Miss Evans?

MARY ANN. No, nothing at all. We are quite finished.

Pause. BARING *places his copy of the will back into his briefcase.*

BARING. You can keep your copy of the will, Miss Evans. And Mr Evans, I believe you have yours already.

ISAAC. More than one, yes I do.

BARING. Very good. In that case I shall take my leave.

MARY ANN. Thank you, Mr Baring. I hope you enjoy your dinner.

ISAAC. I will show you out.

ISAAC *stands and the two men start to make their way towards the door. But then,* BARING *pauses, and turns to* MARY ANN.

BARING. May I say, you are a formidable woman, Miss Evans. And at least, you have the experience.

MARY ANN. Experience?

BARING. Of work, I mean. Of paid work. Not many women can say that. So, despite the fact that your situation has been revealed to be perhaps more precarious than you had hoped for, you do have a history of being remunerated for your labour.

ISAAC. Mary Ann's ambition is to be a writer.

BARING. I'm sure you will have a lot to say.

MARY ANN. For the time being, I have had to do translating work, but the payments are modest.

BARING. Ah, yes, my wife pointed it out to me in *The Birmingham Journal*, one day. There was an article about this book you translated?

FOUR 97

MARY ANN. I saw the article.

ISAAC. We all did.

BARING. Quite a story. What was the book's title, again, I don't recall it.

MARY ANN. *Das Leben Jesu: kritisch bearbeitet.*

BARING. I do not speak German.

MARY ANN. *The Life of Jesus: Critically Examined.*

BARING. And you were working on it here, in this house?

MARY ANN. In this very room, sometimes. It took me four years and it was very draining.

BARING. I am not in the least bit surprised. I understand, that apart from your fluent German, you even learnt Hebrew during the onerous task of translating this book.

MARY ANN. I believe in doing a job thoroughly, Mr Baring.

BARING. Formidable, formidable.

Pause.

And this man, the writer.

MARY ANN. David Friedrich Strauss.

BARING. Is it true that he has been quite pilloried in his own country?

MARY ANN. It is, yes.

BARING. Hated. Vilified.

ISAAC. Rightly so.

BARING. Because of the subject of the book, is that correct? My wife mentioned it has something to do with discrediting Christianity.

MARY ANN. Your wife is wrong, Mr Baring.

BARING. Demystifying it then, degrading it.

Pause.

A strange choice of book to translate, Miss Evans, if you don't mind me saying. A strange choice.

Pause.

And to think your father was dying in that very bed as you scribbled away.

Pause.

Goodnight to you.

But she stops him.

MARY ANN. No, sir. I have something to say to you. Please, stay.

BARING. I beg your pardon?

MARY ANN. I said, stay.

ISAAC. Mary Ann.

MARY ANN. What is it, Isaac?

ISAAC. Mr Baring needs to leave.

MARY ANN. No, he will stay until I have spoken.

BARING *and* ISAAC *look at each other, bewildered by the turn in her. In the parlour room,* MARIA *has put down her knitting; she edges her way into the hallway, in order to be closer, and listen from the other side of the door.*

Will you please convey a message to your wife, for me. And perhaps you may find it useful yourself.

BARING. What is the message?

ISAAC. Mary Ann.

MARY ANN. I will speak, Isaac.

She walks over to the bookcase, scans the shelves with her eyes, picks out the biggest book. It is Robert's Bible; she holds it in her hands.

Tell her, if you please, that to question the historical veracity of a text, is not to discredit it. In the case we speak of, the motive perhaps is simply to interrogate something of the way that particular text has been turned into a monolithic force that shackles and binds us.

BARING. That is sacrilegious, madam.

MARY ANN. The sacrilege, sir, is in those who take a tale of wonder and awe about what it means to be a human being and turn it into a mere harness. Tell her please, that in order to find the meaning of Jesus walking on water in Galilee, we do not need proof of the date and time of the event, or the temperature of the water on the particular day. It is a vital story, not her recipe for chicken pie.

BARING. Are you finished, Miss Evans?

MARY ANN. For now.

BARING. I am happy to hear it.

Pause.

Goodnight to you.

ISAAC. I will show you out, Mr Baring.

BARING. No need, Mr Evans, I will show myself out.

Just before he leaves the room, he turns to MARY ANN.

I am glad, at least, that your father gets the final word.

And he storms out.

ISAAC. That was not the right way to conduct yourself, Mary Ann.

MARY ANN. Please refrain from giving me lessons in behaviour.

ISAAC. There is no question in my mind that Father's will was influenced by your work on that blasted book.

MARY ANN. You are probably right.

Pause.

ISAAC. Anyway, I am sorry it was not quite what you were hoping for.

Pause.

But I shall help you, Mary Ann. You will not be allowed to starve.

MARY ANN. How kind.

Pause.

ISAAC. There is something else.

MARY ANN. Oh?

ISAAC. I will of course be selling Bird Grove. Sarah and I will remain at Griff House, so to own two houses does not make any sense at all.

MARY ANN. I can see that.

ISAAC. So, I shall be selling it.

Pause.

In fact, I have found a buyer. It is most fortunate. It is through Peter Jessop, do you remember him? It is for his cousin, who is moving to the area. By sheer coincidence, he knows the house well because he had stayed in it when he was a guest of the previous owners. He is very keen to buy it and he is offering a good price.

Pause.

But there is an urgency. His wife is pregnant and they want to move in before their child is born. End of September, they were hoping for.

MARY ANN. But I am travelling to the Continent tomorrow, with the Brays, and I will not be back till November at the earliest.

Pause. A stand-off.

ISAAC. I will make sure that all of your belongings are taken away and stored safely at Griff House during your absence. Rest assured.

MARY ANN. So, tonight is the last night.

Pause.

ISAAC. I am sorry. Enjoy your travels.

Pause.

The thing is this, Mary Ann. You may think perhaps that I have not always been the best brother. Maybe. Probably. But let me say this.

Pause, he waits for the words, wanting to make sure they are the correct ones.

We live in this world, not another. And within the confines of this particular world, within its constrictions, its rules, its obligations, I have always tried to do my best by you. So, do not condemn me. I do my best, Mary Ann, I do my best.

MARY ANN. Only you know if you do. But, I am not your confessor, Isaac. I am your sister.

Pause. And then he leaves.

MARY ANN *is left alone in the study.*

For a few seconds, she paces around the room in something of a daze, as if trying to absorb everything she has heard over the last few minutes.

She looks down into her hands and realises she is still holding the Bible.

Then she is drawn back to the bookshelves. She looks at the titles, at the writers. She looks at the Bible, that she is still holding, rests it down.

Then she takes out another book, opens it.

Walter Scott.

She drops it to the floor with some force. Takes out another one.

Daniel Defoe.

Drops it to the floor. Takes out another.

Jonathan Swift.

Drops it to the floor. Another. With a bit more force.

Henry Fielding.

Throws it to the floor. Another.

Horace Walpole.

Throws it. Another.

Thomas Paine.

Throws it. Another.

John Donne.

Then she returns to the Bible, picks it up again. For a second she hesitates, but then, she suddenly brings it high above her head, and throws that too, violently to the floor.

She then walks to her father's bed. She stands over it, looks down at it, as if trying to work something out.

She slowly sits on the edge of the bed; she remains there for a few seconds.

And then she pummels it violently with her fists.

Eventually, exhausted by the exertion, she collapses onto the floor, by the bed.

A few seconds pass. There is a gentle knock on the door. MARY ANN *quickly stands up, composes herself.*

Come in.

The door opens, MARIA *steps in.*

MARIA. It is time for me to leave, Mary Ann.

MARY ANN. Of course, my dear. And you were kind to come and help me pack.

MARIA. You will be seeing the world!

MARY ANN. Well, a small part of it, but it will make a change from Coventry.

MARIA. And you will be staying at the Brays tonight?

MARY ANN. I shall. We are leaving before dawn for Dover.

MARIA *has stepped further into the room; she notices all the books on the floor.*

MARIA. Oh, dear.

MARY ANN. Ah, yes, there was an accident.

MARIA. I understand.

There is a moment; it is clear that MARIA *heard everything.*

Shall I help you tidy them up?

MARY ANN. Thank you, Miss Lewis.

The two women walk over to the pile of books on the floor and start to pick them up one by one, putting them back on the shelves.

I was being petulant. Childish.

MARIA. No. No, you weren't.

They continue picking up the books, and returning them to the shelves.

It was your father who arranged for you to use the library at Arbury Hall when you were a child. Do you remember? He went and begged Mrs Newdigate to let you in, she was most perplexed.

MARY ANN. That's right, she was.

MARIA. An eight-year-old girl who wanted to devour books as if they were sweets. So he would take you there, with her permission, and drop you off every Saturday morning, and then pick you up in the evening, and he did it without fail, every Saturday, year in and year out. And Mrs Newdigate's jaw remained on the floor, she hadn't realised that books were for reading.

Pause.

But it was your father who did that.

MARY ANN. It's true.

MARIA. It is worth remembering.

Pause.

But what is the point of giving someone an education if you do not want them to find their own voice?

MARY ANN. I think he did want me to find it, Miss Lewis.

Pause; she is trying to work something out.

But maybe when I did, it frightened him.

MARIA. It is almost seven years since that day when you announced you would no longer be joining him at church.

MARY ANN. It is.

MARIA. Do you remember how I begged and cajoled and pleaded with you not to do it?

MARY ANN. I do.

MARIA. I was frightened too.

Pause.

Sometimes I think what we are most frightened of is our own awakening.

She walks over to MARY ANN, *kisses her on the forehead.*

Goodbye, my love.

MARY ANN. Goodbye, Miss Lewis.

And she leaves the room.

MARY ANN *is suddenly inspired, taken over by a new thought. With renewed energy, she leans down, opens the trunk, and starts to take the books out, one by one, and place them back onto the shelves, with the other books.*

MARIA *is about to step out of the house, when* CHARLES *is stepping into it; he is in a buoyant mood.*

CHARLES. Ah, Miss Lewis, have you seen the errant wife?

MARIA. She is in the parlour room, Mr Bray. Enjoy France, and Italy, and Switzerland, and thank you for inviting me, I am sorry I declined, but it was not the right time for me.

CHARLES. And when is the right time, Miss Lewis?

But she doesn't have an answer to this.

MARIA. Goodbye.

And she leaves the house. CARA *steps into the hallway from the parlour room.*

CARA. There you are.

CHARLES. Horse and cart are ready. What have you been up to, dear wife?

CARA. I have been listening.

CHARLES. To what?

CARA. To life.

CHARLES. That is intriguing, I long to hear more.

CHARLES *points at* MARY ANN*'s trunks.*

These are for me then, your beast of burden?

CARA. They are.

He starts to pick up the two trunks, but struggles.

Careful with your back, you silly man.

CHARLES. Right, I will load these two onto the cart, and shall return for the one which contains the lady's books. And then we should be off, we have an obscenely early start.

And he stumbles out, almost collapsing under the weight of the two trunks.

CARA *drifts into the study to find* MARY ANN *emptying the trunk of its books.*

CARA. What are you doing?

MARY ANN. I shall not be taking this trunk with me, I have read enough for the time being.

CARA. But what will you do with all that free time?

MARY ANN. I will be thinking, Cara. And planning.

CARA. Planning what?

MARY ANN. How I shall earn my living. My father gave me the finest education, I am to use it. First, he led me to books. And today, he taught me something else.

CARA. And what is that?

MARY ANN. That the breadwinner will always choose the bread we eat. So, I shall be making my own.

The books are all on the shelves; MARY ANN *closes the trunk, pushes it to the side of the room.*

Now. I need to close the house up. I mean board up the windows. Cara, will you help me?

CARA. Of course, my dear.

MARY ANN. Let us start in the dining room.

They step into the dining room and together they begin closing all the shutters, so that the house incrementally becomes darker.

CARA. Will you miss Bird Grove?

MARY ANN. I suspect so. But maybe being kicked out is a blessing.

CARA. You have been treated most unfairly.

MARY ANN. I can't disagree.

CARA. My blood was boiling for you. Especially that awful solicitor.

Job done in the dining room, MARY ANN *leads the way.*

MARY ANN. And now the parlour room!

She heads into the parlour room, CARA *follows; they do the same there, they close the shutters one by one.*

CARA. You will, of course, be fine, I am not worried about you.

MARY ANN. I'll do my best. But, I am determined.

CARA. Certainly.

MARY ANN. I have ideas.

CARA. Of course you do. Forwards then!

The shutters in the parlour room are all closed.

MARY ANN. Kitchen!

They leave the parlour room and are crossing the hallway on their way to the kitchen, when CHARLES *walks back into the house.*

CHARLES. And now for the books. Where are they, Miss Evans?

MARY ANN. They are not joining us.

CARA. Perhaps there are new ones to be written.

CHARLES. I am confused.

CARA. Wait for us in the carriage, Charles. We shall join you in a moment.

CHARLES. Bewildered.

CARA. Go!

CHARLES. Hurry then! We should be up with the sparrows!

And he leaves the house.

MARY ANN *strides purposefully into the kitchen, with* CARA *in tow.*

They start closing the shutters in there, as well.

MARY ANN. You were right.

CARA. I usually am. But, to what are you referring?

MARY ANN. We stood in this room, years ago, and you urged me to write. You told me to grapple the pen from their hands.

CARA. I am hoping that that is the act you are embarking on.

MARY ANN. I doubt they will enjoy sharing the storytelling.

CARA. It is not their natures that hinder them. It is the force of habit.

MARY ANN. Or maybe a little of both. But there is no going back!

Shutters are all closed in the kitchen; she heads for the door.

Study!

MARY ANN *and* CARA *enter the final room, the study, and they get going on the shutters in there.*

CARA. And your father?

MARY ANN. What about him?

CARA. Will you forgive him, Mary Ann?

MARY ANN. We will have to wait and see.

They close all the shutters. The only light that now enters the house is the evening sun that comes through the open front door.

CARA. But there is something that I have wanted to ask you for a long time.

MARY ANN. What is it?

CARA. Do you regret the compromise you made?

MARY ANN. What compromise?

CARA. You went back to church with him. You didn't pray and you didn't sing, but you went back to church with him.

MARY ANN *stops for a beat, thinks of the answer before she speaks it.*

MARY ANN. I imagined myself into his life, and then, yes, I reached across the chasm of our differences before it became unbridgeable.

CARA. But did he do the same?

MARY ANN. Not as much as I would have liked.

CARA. So, why should you be the one who extends her arm?

MARY ANN *considers this.*

MARY ANN. It is who I am. I cannot be what I am not.

CARA. But the world needs to change, Mary Ann.

MARY ANN. Indeed, it does. And we need our fighters, and our rebels, and our flag-bearers. But I believe, Cara, that the greatest and most lasting part of that change will come from listening to each other. Otherwise, what kind of hellish world will we live in?

CARA. That imagining, and that listening. They are love, are they not?

MARY ANN. A substantial part of it.

CARA. It is the same love with which you will write.

Pause.

I am beginning to see, Mary Ann, that love is not a feeling. We have been told so, to undermine its power.

MARY ANN. What is it then?

CARA. An intelligence.

Pause.

MARY ANN. We are done. Thank you for helping me.

CARA. You are welcome. Charles is waiting for us.

MARY ANN. Which is why we should go and join him. But I will need a minute. There is something I have to do before I go.

CARA. Of course. We shall be outside.

CARA *goes, through the hallway, and leaves the house.*

MARY ANN *is alone.*

She edges her way through the dark to Robert's desk and finds a box of matches and a candle; she lights it.

Then, candle in hand, she starts to wander around Bird Grove.

She walks from the study into the hallway. From the hallway, she looks into the dining room, and kitchen.

And then she drifts into the parlour room.

She stands in the middle of the parlour room, looking around the room.

Then, out of nowhere, there is a strange WOMAN *standing at the parlour-room door; we have not seen her before. She is in her late twenties.*

WOMAN. Hello.

Startled, MARY ANN *turns and faces her.*

MARY ANN. Who are you?

WOMAN. I was born in this house.

MARY ANN. I do not understand.

Pause.

WOMAN. You will be published. And you will find your soulmate, too. You will take a man's name, George Eliot, because you know something of the times you live in. You will write seven novels, one of which many believe is the greatest of the nineteenth century.

The WOMAN *is about to step out of the room, but turns back.*

I'm Dorothea, by the way. I live in a town, nearby.

MARY ANN. Which one?

DOROTHEA. Middlemarch.

MARY ANN. I do not know it.

DOROTHEA. You will.

Pause.

Now say your goodbyes, and join us.

And she leaves the house.

Left alone, MARY ANN *steps into Robert's study. She walks around the room, candle in hand. Then, she turns and looks at Robert's bed. She sits down on it, touches it gently, as if remembering.*

Then she stands, looks one last time around the study, taking it all in for the very last time.

MARY ANN. Goodbye, Father.

She blows out the candle, places it on the desk, strides out of the study, across the hallway, through the front door, out of Bird Grove, and into her brilliant future.

The End.

www.nickhernbooks.co.uk

@nickhernbooks